Scottish F_____d___
Street _

CONTEN

Area of Coverage	2-3	Kel	'
Berwick-upon-Tweed	4-7	Langholm, Lauder & indices	9
Canonbie, Chirnside & indices	8-9	Lockerbie & index	30-31
Coldingham, Coldstream,	10-11	Melrose & index	32-33
Cornhill-on-Tweed & indices		Moffat, Newcastleton & indices	34-35
Duns, Earlston & indices	12-13	Newton St Boswells, St Boswells & index	36-37
Eyemouth, Gordon & indices	14-15	Peebles & index	38-39
Galashiels	16-19	Selkirk, St Abbs & indices	40-41
Greenlaw, Hawick & indices	20-23	Walkerburn & index, Berwick-upon-	42-44
Innerleithen, Jedburgh & index	24-25	Tweed & Galashiels indices	

KEY TO MAP SYMBOLS

A74(M)	Motorway	●●●●	Antonine wall (course of)	
A1	Primary route dual / single	P F	Parking / filling station	
A698	A road dual / single	PO L	Post office / library	
B6461	B road dual / single	H S	Hospital / superstore	
	Unclassified road	B i	Bus station / tourist information centre	
	Pedestrian street	Y a	Castle / antiquity	
	Track / path	⌂ ✳	Historic house / garden	
	Town wall	m ⬔	Museum / viewpoint	
	Long distance footpath	⚠ ⬚	Camping / caravan site	
	Railway and station	✳ ✝	Other tourist attraction / church	
	National border		Woodland / recreation or cemetery	
⚑ ⚑ ⚑	Police / fire / ambulance station		Built-up area / water	
⚑ ⚑	Coastguard / lifeboat station		Shingle / sand	
▲ ▼ △	Primary / secondary / special school		Rocks / mud	

Scale 1:14 000

```
0                          500m
|----+----+----+----+----|
0                        500yds
```

ISBN 978 1 86097 381 9

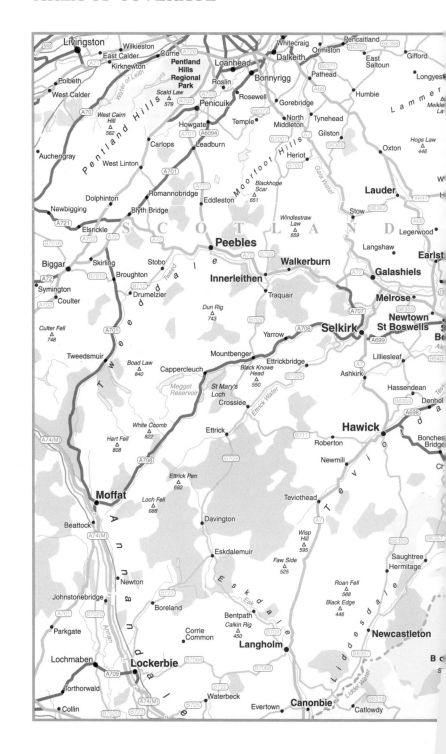

Bogend

A   **B**   **C**   **D**

To Eyemouth
A1(T)

1

Conundrum

Grand

East
Hope

Loaning

Camphill
Cotts

Meadow
House In

2

Camphill

Mast

Mast

Halidon
Hill

Mast

P

A6105
To Duns

D U N S

R O A D

Halidon
Terr

Reservoir

Meadow
Hill

3

Nine Well
Eyes

Meadow
Hill
House

A6105

DUNS RD

Grange Road

The
Elms

CAST

Road

Castlehills
Lodge

4

Letham
Shank

High
Letham

Castlehills
Farm

BERWICK-UPON-TWEE

Paxton

Myecroft

Castlehills
House

Lower
Pool

5

Chateau
Pedro

High
Pool

A1(T)

A   **B**   6   **C**

Yarrow
Slake

D

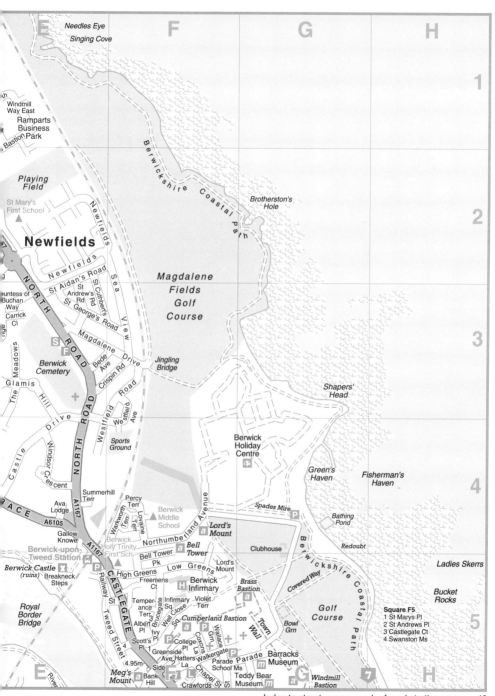

5

E Needles Eye
Singing Cove

F

G

H

1

Windmill
Way East

Ramparts
Business
Park

Bastion

Berwickshire Coastal Path

Playing
Field

Brotherston's
Hole

2

St Mary's
First School

Newfields

Newfields

Countess of
Buchan
Way

Carrick
Cl

NORTH ROAD

St Aidan's Road

St
Andrew's
Rd

St Cuthbert's Rd

St George's Road

Sea View

Magdalene
Fields
Golf
Course

3

The Meadows

Glamis

Hill

Drive

Castle

Windsor Crescent

Magdalene Drive

Bede
Ave

Crispin Rd

Berwick
Cemetery

Westfield Road

Westfield
Ave

Jingling
Bridge

Shapers'
Head

Sports
Ground

Berwick
Holiday
Centre

Green's
Haven

Fisherman's
Haven

4

TERRACE

A6105

Summerhill
Terr

Ava
Lodge

A1167

Gallow
Knowe

Percy
Terr

Warkworth Terr

Lovaine
Terr

Berwick
Middle
School

Northumberland Avenue

Spades Mire

Bathing
Pond

Redoubt

Berwick-upon-
Tweed Station

Berwick
Holy Trinity
First Sch.

Bell Tower
Pk

Bell
Tower

Lord's
Mount

Clubhouse

Lord's
Mount

Berwickshire Coastal Path

Ladies Skerrs

Berwick Castle
(ruins)

Breakneck
Steps

CASTLEGATE

Railway

High Greens

Freemens
Ct

Low Greens

Berwick
Infirmary

Brass
Bastion

Covered Way

Golf
Course

Bucket
Rocks

5

Royal
Border
Bridge

Tweed Street

Temper-
ance
Terr

Albert
Pl

Scott's
Pl

Infirmary
Sq

Violet
Terr

Cumberland Bastion

Ivy
Pl

College
Pl

Coxons

Wallace Grn

Greenside
Ave

Walkergate
La

Parade

Town Wall

Bowl
Grn

Barracks
Museum

Square F5
1 St Marys Pl
2 St Andrews Pl
3 Castlegate Ct
4 Swanston Ms

Meg's
Mount

4.95m

Bank
Hill

Side

Chapel St

Crawfords

Parade
School Ms

Teddy Bear
Museum

Windmill
Bastion

River

E

7

G

H

Index to street names can be found starting on page 42

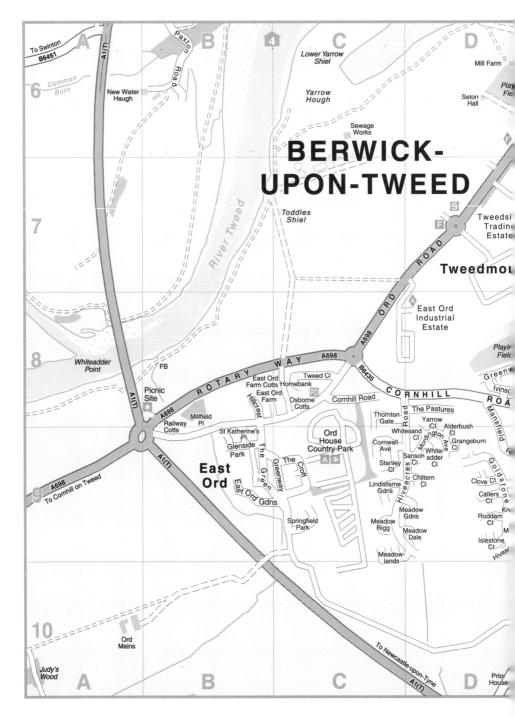

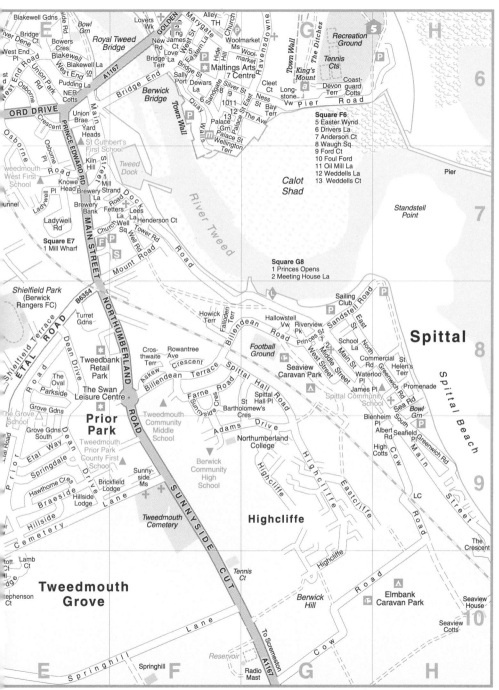

Blakewell Gdns
Bowl Grn
Royal Tweed Bridge
Bowers Cres
Blakewell
Blakewell La
Bridge Ct
West End Pl
West End Rd
Union Park
West End St
Pudding La
NER Cotts
Berwick Bridge
GOLDEN
Lovers Wk
New James Rd
Ct
Love La
Bridge La
Terr
Sally Port
Dewars La
Alley
TH
Church
Maryate
Woolmarket Ms
Wool-market
Silver St
Sandgate
9
10 11
12
13
Palace Grn
Palace St
Wellington Terr
Haversdowne
Town Wall
The Ditches
Recreation Ground
Tennis Cts
King's Mount
Cleet Ct
Long-stone
Ness St
Devon Terr
Coast-guard Cotts
Pier Bay Terr
The Ave
Road

Ord Drive
Prince Edward Rd
Union Brae
Yard Heads
St Cuthbert's First School
Kiln Hill
Mill
Brewery La
Brewery Bank
Fetters La
Lees La
Henderson Ct
Strand Road
Knowe Head
Ladywell Pl
Ladywell Rd
Church Sq
Well La
Tower Rd
Weir Rd

Square F6
5 Easter Wynd
6 Drivers La
7 Anderson Ct
8 Waugh Sq
9 Ford Ct
10 Foul Ford
11 Oil Mill La
12 Weddells La
13 Weddells Ct

Calot Shad

Pier

Square E7
1 Mill Wharf

Mount Road

Standstell Point

Square G8
1 Princes Opens
2 Meeting House La

Shielfield Park
(Berwick Rangers FC)
B6354
Turret Gdns
Tweedbank Retail Park
The Swan Leisure Centre
The Oval
Parkside
Grove Gdns
Grove Gdns South

Dean Drive
Etal Road
Shielfield Terrace
Northumberland Road

Prior Park

Tweedmouth Community Middle School
Tweedmouth Prior Park County First School
Brickfield Lodge
Hillside Lodge
Sunnyside Ms
Sunnyside Cut

Howick Terr
Fallodien Terr
Billendean Road
Crosthwaite Terr
Rowantree Ave
Crescent
Askew
Billendean Terrace
Farne Road
Sunnyside Cres
Adams
Spittal Hall Road

Hallowstell Vw
Riverview Pk
Princes St
Football Ground
Seaview Caravan Park
Spittal Hall Pl
St Bartholomew's Cres
Drive
Northumberland College

Sailing Club
Sandstell Road
West Side
Middle Street
Main St
School La
Commercial Rd
Waterloo Pl
James Pl
Spittal Community School
North Greenwich Rd
St Helen's Terr
Promenade
Sea Rd
Bowl Grn
Blenheim Pl
Albert Rd
High Cotts
Seafield Pl
Greenwich Rd

Spittal

Spittal Beach

South Main Street

Berwick Community High School
Tweedmouth Cemetery

Highcliffe

Highcliffe
Eastcliffe Road
Berwick Hill
LC
Cow Road

The Crescent

Lamb Ct
Stephenson Ct

Tweedmouth Grove

Tennis Ct
Springhill Lane
Reservoir
Radio Mast
Springhill

Berwick Hill
Elmbank Caravan Park
Cow Road
Seaview House
Seaview Cotts

River Tweed

Maltings Arts 7 Centre
Town Wall
Quay Walls
Tweed Dock

Etal Way
Springdale
Hawthorne Cres
Braeside
Hillside Lane
Hillside Cemetery

A1167

Index to street names can be found starting on page 42

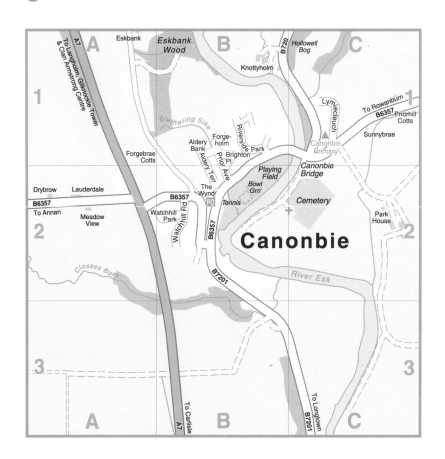

Index to Canonbie

Aldery Bank	B1
Aldery Terrace	B2
Brighton Place	B1
Forgebrae Cottages	A1
Forgeholm	B1
Lymiecleuch	C1
Prior Avenue	B1
Priorhill Cottages	C1
Riverside Park	B1
Watchhill Park	B2
Watchhill Road	B2
Wynd, The	B2

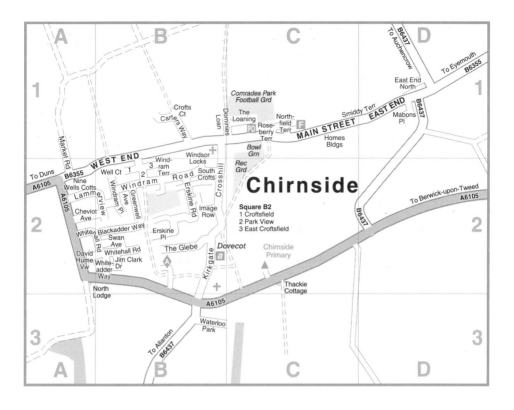

Index to Chirnside

Blackadder Way	B2	Greenwell Avenue	B2	Roseberry Terrace	C1
Carters Way	B1	Homes Buildings	C1	Smiddy Terrace	C1
Cheviot Avenue	A2	Image Row	B2	South Crofts	B2
Crofts Court	B1	Jim Clark Drive	B2	Swan Avenue	B2
Croftsfield (1)	B2	Kirkgate	B2	Waterloo Park	B3
Crosshill	B2	Lammerview	A2	Well Court	B2
David Hume View	A2	Loaning, The	C1	West End	A2
Dominies Loan	B1	Mabons Place	D1	Whiteadder	B2
East Croftsfield (3)	B2	Main Street	C1	Way	
East End	D1	Market Road	A1	Whitehall Road	A2, B2
East End North	D1	Nine Wells	A2	Windram Place	B2
Erskine Place	B2	Cottages		Windram Road	B2
Erskine Road	B2	Northfield Terrace	C1	Windram Terrace	B2
Glebe, The	B2	Park View (2)	B2	Windsor Locks	B1

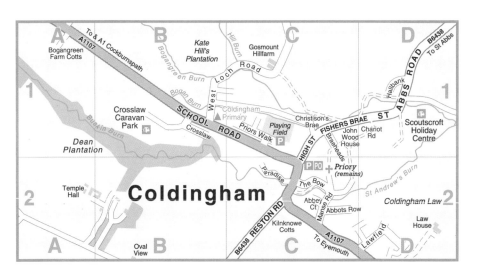

Coldingham

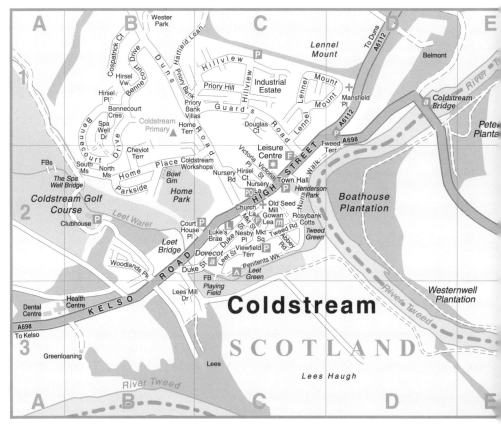

Coldstream

SCOTLAND

Index to Coldingham

Abbey Court	C2
Abbots Row	C2
Bogangreen Farm Cottages	A1
Bow, The	C2
Braeheads	C1
Chariot Road	D1
Christison's Brae	C1
Crosslaw	B1
Fishers Brae	C1
Hallbank	D1
High Street	C2
John Wood House	C1
Kilknowe Cottages	C2
Lawfield	D2
Manse Road	C2
Paradise	C2
Priors Walk	C1
Reston Road	C2
St Abbs Road	D1
School Road	B1
West Loch Road	B1

Index to Coldstream & Cornhill on Tweed

Abbey Road	C2
Bennecourt Crescent	B1
Bennecourt Drive	B1
Cheviot Terrace	B2
Cospatrick Court	B1
Court House Place	B2
Church Lane	C2
Douglas Court	C1
Duke Street	B2, C2
Duns Road	B1
Gowan Lea	C2
Green Lane	G2
Guard's Road	C1
Hatfield Loan	B1
High Street	C2
Hillview	C1
Hirsel Court	C2
Hirsel Place	B1
Hirsel View	B1
Home Place	B2
Home Terrace	B1
Kelso Road	B3
Knowehead	F3
Lees Mill Drive	B3
Leet Street	C2
Lennel Mount	C1
Luke's Brae	C2
Main Street	F3
Mansfield Place	D1
Market Square	C2
Market Street	C2
Milestone Cottages	F3
Nesby Place	C2
North Mews	B2
Nuns Walk	C2
Nursery Lane	C2
Nursery Road	C2
Old Seed Mill	C2
Parkside	B2
Penitents Walk	C2
Priory Bank	B1
Priory Bank Villas	B1
Priory Hill	C1
Rosybank Cottages	C2
St Helens Gardens	F3
Sidings, The	G2
South Mews	B2
Spa Well Drive	B1
Station Cottages	G2
Station Gardens	G3
Tweed Meadows	G3
Tweed Road	C2
Tweed Terrace	C1
Victoria Place	C2
Victoria Street	C2
Viewfield Terrace	C2
Woodlands Park	B2

Cornhill Castle (site of)

Hill Plantation

ENGLAND

To Berwick-upon-Tweed

To The Sidings

Green La

Gdns

Station Cotts

Station Cotts

Cornhill on Tweed

Cornhill County First School

Cornhill Farm

To Wooler

St Helens Gdns

Milestone Cotts

Tweed Meadows

STREET

Sewage Works

MAIN

Cornhill House

To Wark

B6350

Knowehead

Cem

The Old Mill

Bathingwell Plantation

Coppenny Plantation

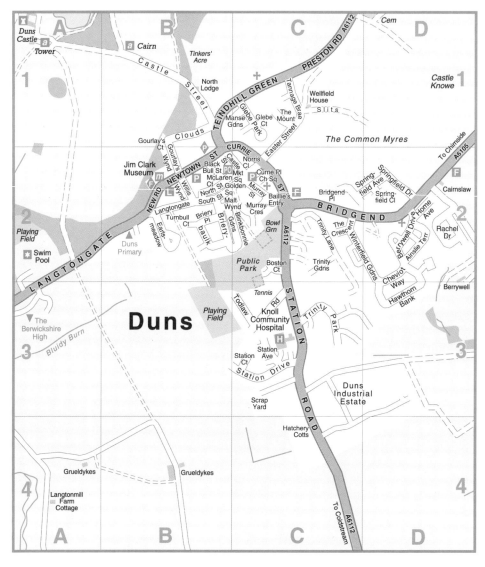

Duns

Index to Duns

		Bridgend Place	C2	Earlsmeadow	B2	Home Avenue	D2
		Briery Place	B2	Easter Street	C2	Langtongate	A3, B2
Ainslie Terrace	D2	Brierybaulk	B2	Glebe Court	C1	McLaren Court	B2
Bailie's Entry	C2	Castle Street	B1, B2	Glebe Park	C1	Malt Wynd	B2
Berrywell Drive	D2	Cheviot Way	D2	Golden Square	B2	Manse Gardens	C1
Black Bull Street	B2	Church Square	C2	Gourlay's Court	B1	Market Square	C2
Blinkbonnie		Clouds	B1	Gourlay's Wynd	B2	Mount, The	C1
Gardens	C2	Crescent, The	C2	Hatchery	C4	Murray Crescent	C2
Boston Court	C2	Currie Place	C2	Cottages		Murray Street	C2
Bridgend	C2	Currie Street	C2	Hawthorn Bank	D3	New Road	B2

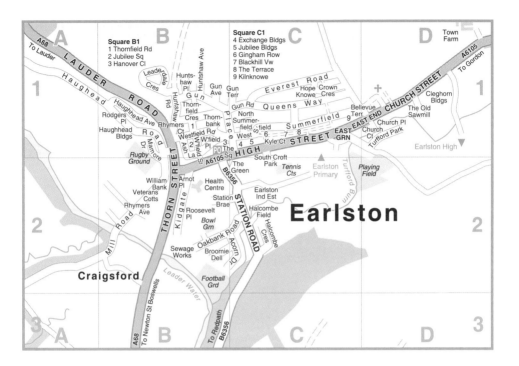

Newtown Street	B2	**Index to Earlston**	
Norris Close	C2		
North Street	B2	Acorn Drive	C2
Preston Road	C1	Arnot Place	B2
Rachel Drive	D2	Ash Lane	B1
Slits	C1	Bellevue Terrace	C1
Springfield Avenue	D2	Blackhill View (7)	C1
Springfield Close	D2	Broomie Dell	B2
Springfield Drive	D2	Church Court	D1
South Street	B2	Church Place	D1
Station Avenue	C3	Church Street	D1
Station Court	C3	Cleghorn Buildings	D1
Station Drive	C3	Crown Crescent	C1
Station Road	C3	East End	C1
Tannage Brae	C1	East Green	C1
Teindhill Green	B1	Everest Road	C1
Todlaw Road	C3	Exchange	C1
Trinity Gardens	C2	Buildings (4)	
Trinity Lane	C2	Gingham Row (6)	C1
Trinity Park	C3	Green, The	C2
Turnbull Court	B2	Gun Avenue	B1
Willis Wynd	B2	Gun Place	B1
Winterfield	C2	Gun Road	C1
Gardens		Gun Terrace	C1

Halcombe Crescent	C2	Old Sawmill, The	D1
Hanover Close (3)	B1	Queens Way	C1
Haughhead Avenue	B1	Rhymer's Court	B1
Haughhead	B1	Rhymers Avenue	B2
Buildings		Roosevelt Place	B2
Haughhead Road	A1	Rodgers Place	B1
High Street	C1	South Crofts Park	C2
Hope Knowe	C1	Square, The	B1
Huntshaw Avenue	B1	Station Brae	B2
Huntshaw Place	B1	Station Road	C2
Huntshaw Road	B1	Summerfield	C1
Jubilee	C1	Terrace, The (8)	C1
Buildings (5)		Thorn Street	B2
Jubilee Square (2)	B1	Thornbank	B1
Kidgate	B2	Thornfield	B1
Kilnknowe (9)	C1	Crescent	
Kyle Court	C2	Thornfield Road (1)	B1
Lauder Road	B1	Turfford Park	D1
Leaderdale	B1	Veterans Cottages	B2
Crescent		West Summerfield	C1
Mamore Drive	B1	Westfield Place	B1
Mill Road	B2	Westfield Road	B1
North Summerfield	C1	Westfield Street	B1
Oakbank Road	B2	William Bank	B2

 **EYEMOUTH & GORDON**

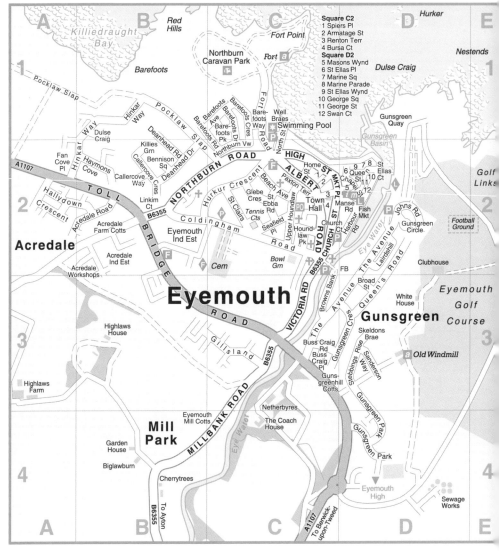

Index to Eyemouth

		Barefoots Avenue	C1	Browns Bank	C3	Deanhead Drive	B
Acredale Farm	B2	Barefoots Crescent	C1	Bursa Court (4)	C2	Deanhead Road	B
Cottages		Barefoots Drive	C1	Buss Craig Place	C3	Dulse Craig	B
Acredale Road	A2	Barefoots Park	C1	Buss Craig Road	C3	Eyemouth Mill	B
Albert Road	C2	Barefoots Road	B1	Callercove Crescent	B2	Cottages	
Armatage	C2	Barefoots Way	C1	Callercove Way	B2	Fan Cove Place	A
Street (2)		Beach Avenue	C2	Chapel Street	D2	Fort Road	C
Avenue, The	D2, C3	Bennison Square	B2	Church Street	C2	George Square (10)	D
		Broad Street	D3	Coldingham Road	C2	George Street (11)	D

15

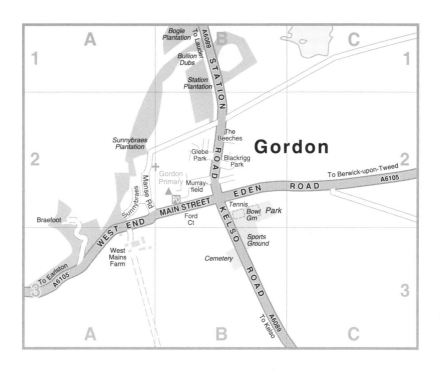

Gordon

Gillsland	C3	Market Place	C2	Victoria Road	C3
Glebe Crescent	C2	Masons Wynd (5)	D2	Well Braes	C1
Gunsgreen Circle	D2	Millbank Road	B4		
Gunsgreen	C3	North Street	C2		
Crescent		Northburn Road	B2	**Index to Gordon**	
Gunsgreen Park	D3, D4	Northburn View	C2		
Gunsgreenhill	C3	Paxton Terrace	C2	Beeches, The	B2
Cottages		Pocklaw Slap	A1, B1	Blackrigg Park	B2
Hallydown	A2	Queen Street	D2	Eden Road	B2
Crescent		Queen's Road	D3	Ford Court	B2
Harbour Road	D2	Renton Terrace (3)	C2	Glebe Park	B2
Haymons Cove	B2	St Clairs	C2	Kelso Road	B2
High Street	C2	St Ebba Road	C2	Main Street	B2
Hinkar Way	A2, B1	St Ellas Court	D2	Manse Road	A2
Home Street	C2	St Ellas Place (6)	D2	Murrayfield	B2
Houndlaw Park	C2	St Ellas Wynd (9)	D2	Station Road	B2
Hurkur Crescent	B2	Sanderson Way	D3	Sunnybraes	A2
Johns Road	D2	Seafield Place	C2	West End	A3
Killies Green	B2	Skeldons Brae	D3		
Lairdshill	D2	Spiers Place (1)	C2		
Linkim Court	B2	Stebbings Rise	D3		
Manse Road	D2	Swan Court (12)	D2		
Marine Parade (8)	D2	Toll Bridge Road	B2		
Marine Square (7)	D2	Upper Houndlaw	C2		

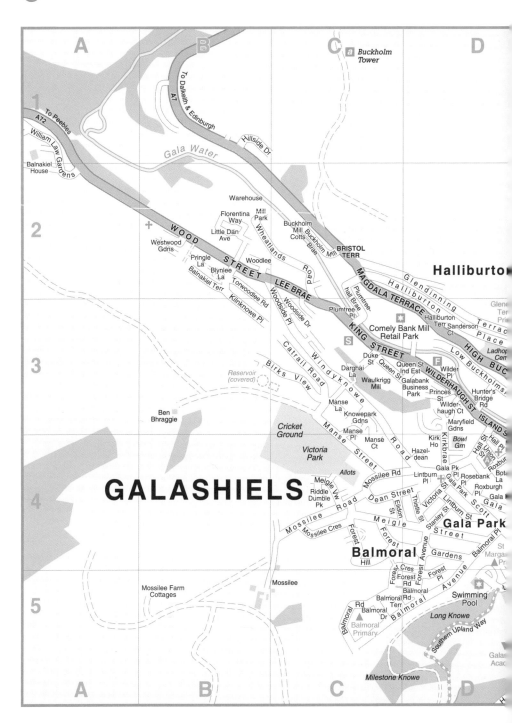

A   **B**   **C**   **D**

a Buckholm Tower

1

To Peebles
A72

William Law Gardens

To Dalkeith & Edinburgh
A7

Balnakiel House

Gala Water

Hillside Dr

2

Warehouse

Florentina Way
Mill Park

Little Dan Ave

Westwood Gdns

Pringle La

Blynlee La

WOOD STREET

Woodlee

Wheatlands Road

Buckholm Mill Cotts
Buckholm Mill
Buckholm Brae

BRISTOL TERR

MAGDALA TERRACE

Glendinning

Halliburton

Halliburto

Balnakiel Terr

Torwoodlee Rd

LEE BRAE

Woodside Dr
Woodside Pl

Plumtree hall Brae

Plumtree Pl

Glene Ter Pri

Klinknowe Pl

KING STREET

Comely Bank Mill Retail Park

Halliburton Terr Sanderson Ct

Terrace Place

3

Reservoir (covered)

Birks View

Catrail Road

Windyknowe

Darghai La

Duke St

Queen St
Queen St Ind Est

Waulkrigg Mill

Galabank Business Park

S

Wilder Pl

WILDERHAUGH ST

Low Buckholms

HIGH BUC

Ladho Cen

F

Hunter's Bridge

Ben Bhraggie

Manse La

Knowepark Gdns

Princes St
Wilder-haugh Ct

ISLAND S

Maryfield Gdns

4

Cricket Ground

Victoria Park

GALASHIELS

Allots

Meigle Vw
Riddle Dumble Pk

Manse St

Manse Pl
Manse Ct

Manse Road

Kirk Ho

Hazel-dean

Kirkbrae

Bowl Grn

St Union

Hall St

Mossilee Rd

Dean Street

Eldon St

Thistle St

Victoria St

Gala Pk Pl
Lintburn Pl

Rosebank Pl

Gala Park Pl

Roxbur

St Hall St

Bot La

Roxburgh Pl
Gala

Mossilee Road

Mossilee Cres

Meigle Street

Forest

Stanley St

Lintburn St

Scott Street

Gala Park

Balmoral Pl

Balmoral
Hill

Forest Avenue

Forest Pl

Gardens

St Marga Pr

5

Mossilee Farm Cottages

Mossilee

Forest Cres
Forest Rd

Balmoral Rd
Terr

Balmoral Rd

Balmoral
Dr

Balmoral Primary

Balmoral Rd

Forest Pl

Balmoral Avenue

Swimming Pool

Long Knowe

Southern Upland Way

Gala Aca

Milestone Knowe

A   **B**   **C**   **D**

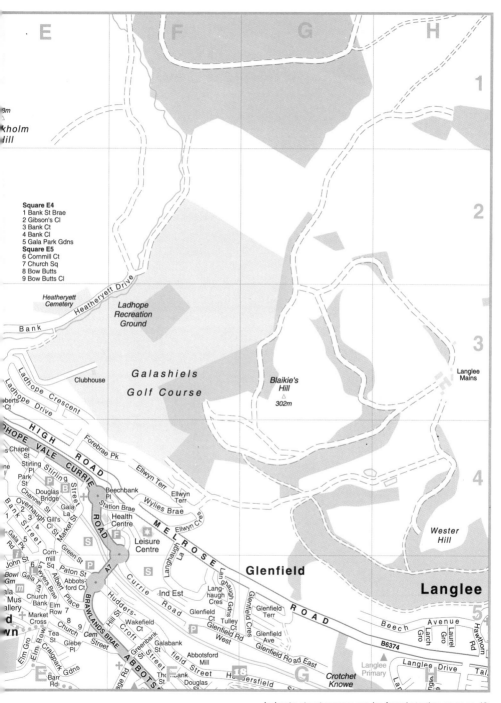

Square E4
1 Bank St Brae
2 Gibson's Cl
3 Bank Ct
4 Bank Cl
5 Gala Park Gdns
Square E5
6 Cornmill Ct
7 Church Sq
8 Bow Butts
9 Bow Butts Cl

Heatheryett Cemetery

Heatheryett Drive

Ladhope Recreation Ground

Bank

Ladhope Crescent

Ladhope Drive

Clubhouse

Galashiels Golf Course

Blaikie's Hill △ 302m

Langlee Mains

HIGH VALE CURRIE ROAD

Forebrae Pk

Ellwyn Terr

Ellwyn Terr

Beechbank Pl

Wylies Brae

Ellwyn Cres

Chapel St
Stirling Pl
Stirling Street
Park St
Douglas Bridge
Channel St
Overhaugh St
Gala La
Gill's Cl
Bank Street
Gala Pk
Gala Rd
Station Brae
Health Centre
Market St
Green St

Leisure Centre

MELROSE

Wester Hill

John St
Cornmill Sq
Paton St
Bowl Grn
Gala Terr
Lawyers Brae
Abbotsford Ct
Albert Pl
Gala Mus
Gallery
Church Bank
Elm Row

Langhaugh La

Ind Est

Glenfield

Langlee

Currie Road

Langhaugh Gdns

Langhaugh Cres

Glenfield Ct

Glenfield Rd West

Tulley Ct

Glenfield Cres

Glenfield Terr

Glenfield Ave

Glenfield Road East

ROAD

Beech Avenue

B6374

Hawthorn Rd
Larch Gro
Laurel Gro

Market Cross
Elm Gro
Tea St
Church St
Craigpark Gdns
Glebe Pl
Barr Rd

BRAWLANDS BRAE

ABBOTS

Hudders-field Croft
Wakefield Ct
Greenbank Ct
Cem Street
Greenbank St
field Street
Galabank St
Abbotsford Mill
Thornbank
Huddersfield St
Douglas

Langlee Primary

Langlee Drive

Tal

Crotchet Knowe

Index to street names can be found starting on page 43

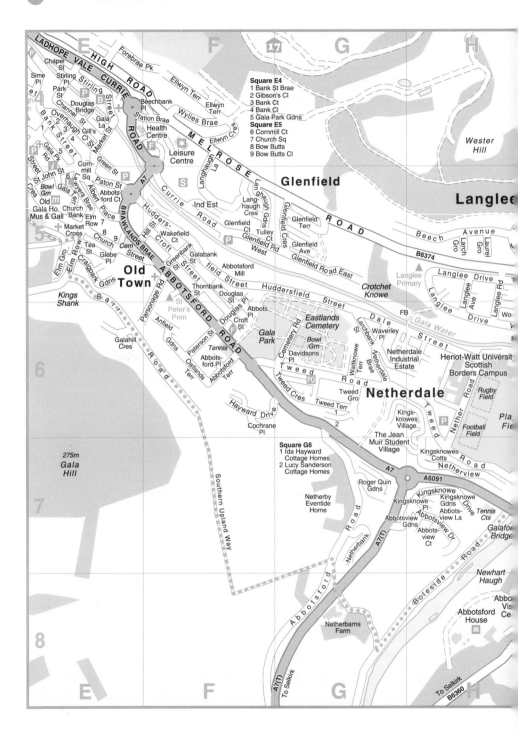

Square E4
1 Bank St Brae
2 Gibson's Cl
3 Bank Ct
4 Bank Cl
5 Gala Park Gdns

Square E5
6 Cornmill Ct
7 Church Sq
8 Bow Butts
9 Bow Butts Cl

Square G6
1 Ida Hayward
  Cottage Homes
2 Lucy Sanderson
  Cottage Homes

Glenfield

Langlee

Old Town

Netherdale

Gala Hill

275m
Gala Hill

Kings Shank

Eastlands Cemetery

Gala Park

Heriot-Watt University
Scottish Borders Campus

Abbotsford House

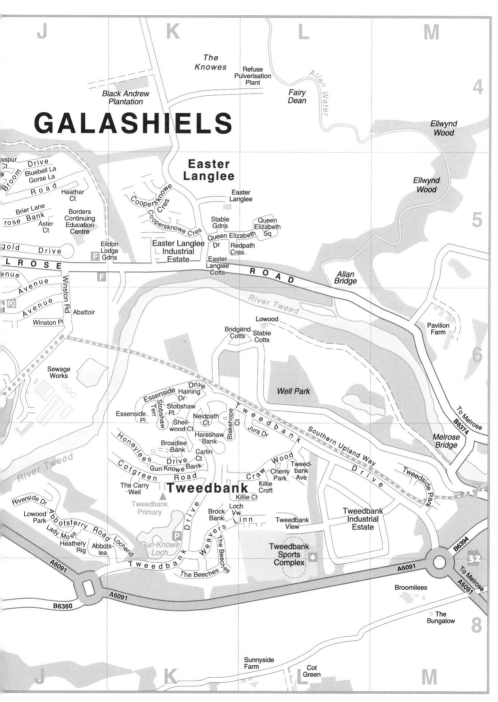

GALASHIELS

The Knowes

Refuse Pulverisation Plant

Fairy Dean

Black Andrew Plantation

Allan Water

Ellwynd Wood

Easter Langlee

Ellwynd Wood

kspur

Drive

Bluebell La

Broom

Gorse La

Road

Heather Ct

Brier Lane

Borders Continuing Education Centre

rose Bank

Aster Ct

Coopersknowe Cres

Coopersknowe Cres

Easter Langlee

Stable Gdns

Queen Elizabeth Sq

jold Drive

Eildon Lodge Gdns

F

Easter Langlee Industrial Estate

Queen Elizabeth Dr

Redpath Cres

LROSE

Easter Langlee Cotts

R O A D

Allan Bridge

nue

F

Avenue

Winston Rd

Abattoir

River Tweed

Lowood

PO

Avenue

Bridgend Cotts

Stable Cotts

Pavilion Farm

Winston Pl

Sewage Works

Drive

Well Park

Haining Dr

Essenside Drive

Stobshaw Pl

Stobshaw Terr

Essenside Pl

Neidpath Ct

Sheil-wood Ct

Hareshaw Bank

Blakehope Ct

Jura Dr

Tweedbank

Southern Upland Way

To Melrose

B6374

Melrose Bridge

Honeylees

Broadlee Bank

Drive

Carlin Ct

Gun Knowes Bank

Cotgreen Road

Wood

Craw

Tweed-bank Ave

Cherry Park

Drive

Tweedside Park

River Tweed

The Carry Weil

Tweedbank Primary

Tweedbank

Killie Croft

Killie Ct

Riverside Dr

Lowood Park

Abbotsferry Road

Lady Moss

Heathery Rig

Abbots-lea

Lochend

Gun Knowe Loch

P

Drive

Brock Bank

Loch Vw

Linn

Weavers

The Beeches

Tweedbank View

Tweedbank Industrial Estate

B6394

A6091

B6360

A6091

Tweedbank

The Beeches

Tweedbank Sports Complex

A6091

Broomilees

32

To Melrose

A6091

The Bungalow

8

Sunnyside Farm

Cot Green

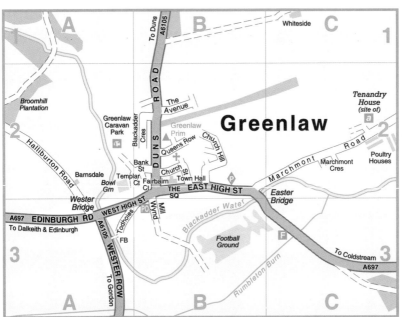

Index to Greenlaw

Avenue, The	B2
Bank Street	B2
Blackadder Crescent	B2
Church Hill	B2
Church Street	B2
Duns Road	B2
East High Street	B2
Edinburgh Road	A3
Fairbairn Court	B2
Halliburton Road	A2
Marchmont Crescent	C2
Marchmont Road	C2
Mill Wynd	B3
Queens Row	B2
Square, The	B2
Templar Court	B2
Todholes	A3
West High Street	A3
Wester Row	A1

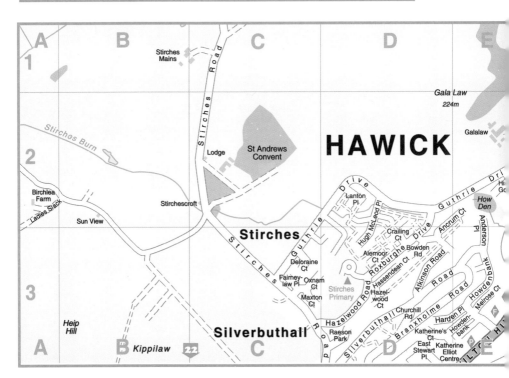

Index to Hawick

Albert Road 22 D5
Alemoor Court 20 D3
Allars Bank 22 D6
Allars Crescent 22 D6
Ancrum Court 20 D2
Anderson Place 20 E2
Appletreehall 21 F2
  Road
Arthur Street 22 E4
Atkinson Road 20 D3
Backdam 22 D6
  Gate (9)
Bailleul Grove 23 F5
Baker Street 22 D5
Bath Street 22 D5
Beaconsfield 22 C6
  Terrace
Beaconsfield 22 C6
  Terrace Lane (2)
Beattie Court 21 F3
Birch Cottages 23 F4
Boonraw Road 21 F2
Borthaugh Road 22 B6
Borthwick Court 21 F2
Borthwick Road 21 F2
Bothwell Court 22 C4

Bourtree Bank 22 D5
Bourtree Place 22 D5
Bourtree 22 E5
  Terrace (1)
Bowden Road 20 D3
Braid Road 22 E6
Branxholme 20 D3
  Road
Bright Street 22 C6
Brougham 22 D5
  Place
Bruce Court 22 C4
Buccleuch 22 C6
  Place (1)
Buccleuch Road 22 B7
Buccleuch 22 C6
  Street
Buccleuch 22 C6
  Terrace
Burnflat Drive 22 B7
Burnflat Lane 22 B7
Burnfoot Road 21 E3
Burnfoot Road 21 G2
Burnhead 21 G2
  Road
Burns Road 21 G2
Carnarvon 22 C5
  Street

Cavers View 21 G2
Charles Street 21 F2
Chay Blyth Place 21 F3
Cheviot Road 22 C6
Church Lane 21 E2
Churchill Road 20 D3
Commercial 22 D5
  Road
Corn Mill Court 22 D6
Crailing Court 20 D3
Croft Road 22 D5
Cross Wynd 22 D5
Crowbyres 22 D8
  Cottages
Crown Close (8) 22 D6
Crumhaugh Hill 22 B7
  Road
Crumhaugh 22 C6
  Road
Dakers Place 22 E5
Dalkeith Place 22 E5
Daykin's Drive 21 G3
Dean Road 22 B5
Deanfield Court 22 C5
Deloraine Court 20 C3
Dickson Court 22 D4
Dickson Street 22 D4
Douglas Haig 22 E5

Court (2)
Douglas Road 22 E5
Douglas Road 23 E4
  East
Dovecot Mews 22 D4
Dovecote Street 22 D4
Dovemount 22 D4
  Place
Drumlanrig 22 D6
  Court
Drumlanrig 22 C6
  Place
Drumlanrig 22 D6
  Square
Duke Street 22 E4
Earl Street 22 E4
East Stewart 20 D3
  Place
Eastfield Road 23 E4
Edina Place 22 E5
Eildon Road 21 F2
Elm Court 22 E6
Elm Grove 22 E6
Ettrick Terrace 22 E5
Fairhurst Drive 21 G3
Fairneylaw 20 C3
  Place
Fenwick Park 23 F4
Fisher Avenue 22 E6
Frank Place (10) 22 D6
Frank Scott 22 C6
  Court
Fraser Avenue 21 F2
Galalaw Road 21 F2
Garfield Street 22 D6
Gladstone 22 C6
  Street
Glebemill 23 E4
  Street
Glebe Place 22 E6
Green Lane 22 C6
Green Terrace 22 C6
Greenheads 22 C6
  Terrace
Greenside Hall 22 C4
  Road
Guthrie Drive 20 C3
Guthrie Drive 20 D2
Haggis Ha'brae 22 B8
Hamilton Road 21 G3
Harden Place 20 D3
Hassendean 20 D3
  Court
Havelock Place 22 D4
Havelock Street 22 D4
Hazelwood 20 D3
  Court
Hazelwood 20 D3
  Road
Henderson Road 21 F2

Heronhill Bank 23 G4
Heronhill Close 23 G4
Heronhill 23 G4
  Crescent
High Street 22 D5
Hillend Drive 21 E2
Hillend Drive 21 E3
Hislop Gardens 20 E2
Howdenbank 20 E3
Howegate 22 D6
Howlands 22 C5
  Terrace
Hugh Mcleod 20 D3
  Place
Hunter Terrace 22 D4
Ivanhoe Terrace 21 E3
Katherine's 20 D3
  Court
Kenilworth 21 F2
  Avenue
Kilmeny 22 C5
Kings Mews 22 D5
Kirk Wynd 22 D6
Kirkstile (4) 22 D6
Ladies Slack 20 A2
Laidlaw Terrace 22 D4
Laing Terrace 22 D4
Langheugh 22 B6
  Road
Langlands Bank 22 C5
Langlands 22 C5
  Court
Langlands 22 C5
  Road
Lanton Place 20 D2
Leaburn Drive 23 F4
Leaburn Grove 23 F5
Leishman Place 21 F2
Leyden Bank 23 F4
Liddesdale 22 C8
  Crescent
Liddesdale 22 C7
  Road
Linden Crescent 22 E5
Linden Terrace 22 E5
Loan 22 C6
Loch Park Road 22 E5
Lockhart Place 22 E5
Lockiesedge 22 D4
Longbaulk Road 22 B7
Longcroft 22 C6
  Crescent
Longcroft Road 22 C6
Longhope Drive 22 B7
Lothian Street 22 D5
Lovel Court (7) 22 D6
McLagan Drive 21 F3
McLaren Court 21 F3
Mansfield 22 E4
  Crescent

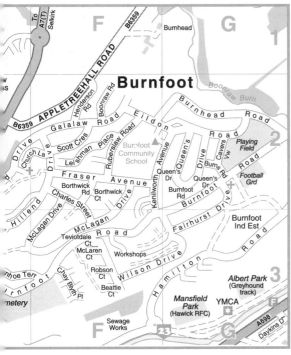

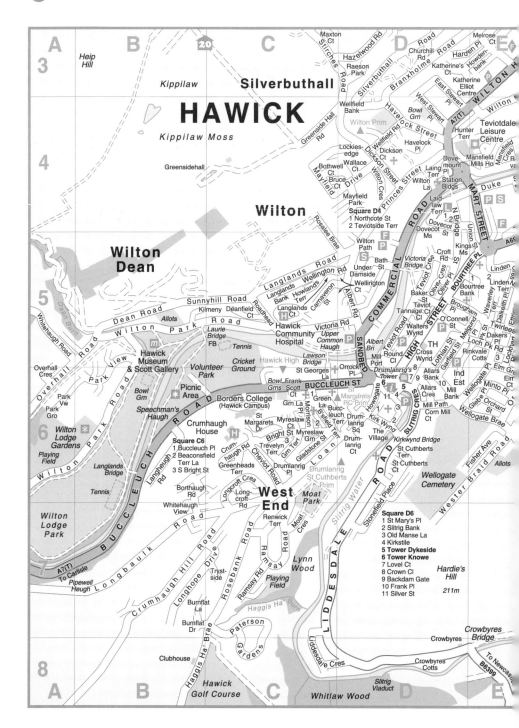

HAWICK

Kippilaw

Silverbuthall

Kippilaw Moss

Greensidehall

Wilton Dean

Wilton

Heip Hill

Square D4
1 Northcote St
2 Teviotside Terr

Square C6
1 Buccleuch Pl
2 Beaconsfield Terr La
3 S Bright St

Square D6
1 St Mary's Pl
2 Slitrig Bank
3 Old Manse La
4 Kirkstile
5 Tower Dykeside
6 Tower Knowe
7 Lovel Ct
8 Crown Cl
9 Backdam Gate
10 Frank Pl
11 Silver St

Hardie's Hill

211m

West End

Wilton Lodge Park

Wilton Lodge Gardens

Hawick Museum & Scott Gallery

Borders College (Hawick Campus)

Hawick Community Hospital

Teviotdale Leisure Centre

Wellogate Cemetery

Crowbyres Bridge

To Newcastle

B6399

Slitrig Viaduct

Whitlaw Wood

Hawick Golf Course

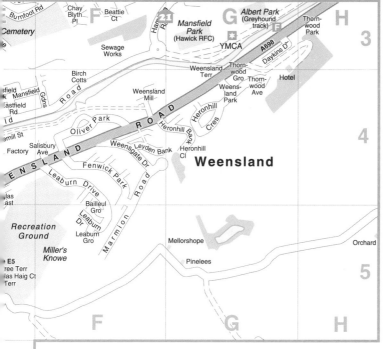

Weensland

Teviotside	22 D4
Terrace (2)	
Thornwood Avenue	23 G4
Thornwood Grove	23 G4
Thornwood Park	23 H3
Tower Dykeside (5)	22 D6
Tower Knowe (6)	22 D6
Trevelyn Terrace	22 C6
Trinity Street	22 E4
Trystside	22 C7
Twirlees Road	22 E5
Twirlees Terrace	22 E5
Under Damside	22 D5
Union Street	22 E4
Victoria Road	22 C5
Village, The	22 D6
Wallace Court	22 D4
Walters Wynd	22 D5
Waverley Terrace	22 E5
Weensgate Drive	23 F4
Weensgate Mill	23 F4
Weensland Park	23 G4
Weensland Road	23 E4
Weensland	23 G4
Terrace	
Wellfield Bank	22 D4
Wellfield Road	22 D4
Wellington Court	22 C5
Wellington Road	22 C5
Wellogate Brae	22 E6
Wellogate Place	22 D6
West Stewart	22 D4
Place	
Wester Braid	22 D7
Road	
Whins Cottage	21 E2
Whitehaugh Road	22 A5
Whitehaugh View	22 B7
Wilson Drive	21 F3
Wilton Crescent	22 D4
Wilton Glebe	20 E3
Wilton Hill	22 E4
Wilton Hill Terrace	22 E4
Wilton Lane	22 E4
Wilton Park Road	22 A6
Wilton Park Road	22 B5
Wilton Path	22 D5
Yarrow Terrace	22 E5

index continued from overleaf...

Mansfield	23 E4	Old Manse	22 D6	Round Close	22 D5
Gardens		Lane (3)		Roxburghe Drive	20 D3
Mansfield Mills	22 E4	Oliver Crescent	22 D5	Ruberslaw Road	21 F2
House		Oliver Park	23 F4	St Cuthberts Court	22 D6
Mansfield Park	23 E4	Oliver Place	22 D5	St Cuthberts	22 D6
Mansfield Road	22 E4	Orchard Street	22 E6	Terrace	
Mansfield Square	22 E4	Orchard Terrace	22 E6	St Georges Lane	22 C6
Marmion Road	23 F5	Orrock Place	22 D6	St Margarets Drive	22 C6
Mart Street	22 E4	Overhall Crescent	22 A6	St Marys Place (1)	22 D6
Maxton Court	20 C3	Overhall Road	22 A6	St Ninians Road	22 E5
Mayfield Drive	22 C4	Oxnam Court	20 C3	Salisbury Avenue	23 F4
Mayfield Park	22 D4	Park Grove	22 A6	Sandbed	22 D5
Melgund Place	22 D5	Park Street	22 E5	Scott Crescent	21 F2
Melrose Court	20 E3	Park Terrace (3)	22 E5	Silver Street (11)	22 D6
Mill Path	22 D6	Park View	22 B6	Silverbuthall Road	20 D3
Mill Port	22 D5	Paterson Gardens	22 C7	Slitrig Bank (2)	22 D6
Minto Place	22 E6	Princes Street	22 D4	Slitrig Crescent	22 D6
Moat Crescent	22 C7	Queen's Drive	21 G2	South Bright	22 C6
Morrison Place	22 C6	Raeson Park	20 D3	Street (3)	
Myreslaw Court	22 C6	Ramsay Road	22 C7	Station Buildings	22 D4
Myreslaw Green	22 C6	Renwick Terrace	22 C7	Stirches Road	20 C2
Noble Place	23 E4	Rinkvale Cottages	22 E5	Stirches Road	20 C3
North Bridge	22 D4	Roadhead	22 C5	Stonefield Place	22 D7
Street		Robson Court	21 F3	Sunnyhill Road	22 C5
Northcote	22 D4	Rosalee Brae	22 C4	Tannage Close	22 D6
Street (1)		Rosebank Road	22 C7	Teviot Court	22 D5
O'Connell Street	22 D5	Rosevale	22 E4	Teviot Crescent	22 D5
		Cottages		Teviot Road	22 D5
		Rosevale Street	22 E4	Teviotdale Court	21 F3

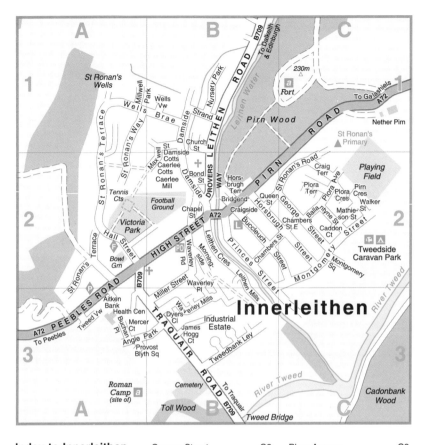

Index to Innerleithen

		George Street	C2	Plora Avenue	C2
		Hall Street	A2	Plora Crescent	C2
Aitken Bank	A3	High Street	B2	Plora Terrace	C2
Angle Park	A3	Horsbrugh Street	B2	Princes Street	B2
Ballantyne Street	C2	Horsbrugh Terrace	B2	Provost Blyth Square	A3
Bond Street	B2	James Hogg Court	B3	Queen Street	B2
Bridgend	B2	Leithen Crescent	B2	St Ronan's Road	C2
Buccleuch Street	B2	Leithen Mills	B2	St Ronan's Terrace	A2
Buchan Place	A3	Leithen Road	B2	St Ronan's Way	A2
Caddon Court	C2	Mathieson Street	C2	Strand	B1
Caerlee Cottages	B2	Maxwell Street	B2	Traquair Road	B3
Chambers Street	B2	Mercer Court	A3	Tweed View	A3
Chambers Street East	C2	Miller Street	B3	Tweedbank Ley	B3
Chapel Street	B2	Millwell Park	A1	Walker Street	C2
Church Street	B1	Montgomery Square	C2	Waverley Mills	B3
Craig Terrace	C2	Montgomery Street	C2	Waverley Place	B2
Craigside	B2	Morningside	B2	Waverley Road	B2
Damside	B1, B2	Nursery Park	B1	Wells Brae	A1
Damside Cottages	B2	Peebles Road	A3	Wells View	B1
Drovers Way	B2	Pirn Crescent	C2		
Dyers Close	B3	Pirn Road	B2		

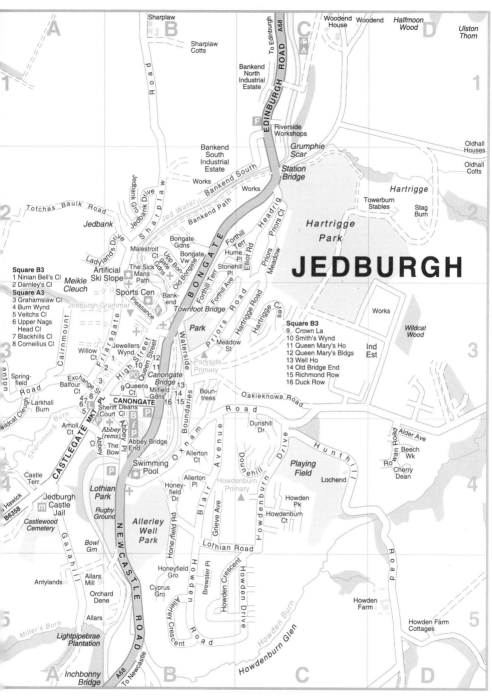

JEDBURGH

Square B3
1 Ninian Bell's Cl
2 Darnley's Cl

Square A3
3 Grahamslaw Cl
4 Burn Wynd
5 Veitchs Cl
6 Upper Nags Head Cl
7 Blackhills Cl
8 Corneilius Cl

Square B3
9 Crown La
10 Smith's Wynd
11 Queen Mary's Ho
12 Queen Mary's Bldgs
13 Well Ho
14 Old Bridge End
15 Richmond Row
16 Duck Row

Sharplaw

Sharplaw Cotts

Woodend House   Woodend   Halfmoon Wood

Ulston Thorn

To Edinburgh   A68   EDINBURGH ROAD

Bankend North Industrial Estate

Riverside Workshops

Grumphie Scar

Oldhall Houses

Oldhall Cotts

Bankend South Industrial Estate

Station Bridge

Hartrigge

Works

Towerburn Stables

Stag Burn

Totches Baulk Road

Jedbank

Bankend South

Works

Hartrigge Park

Jedbank Gro   Jedbank Drive   Sharplaw   Jed Water   Bankend Path   Headrig

Bongate Gdns

Bongate Vw

Malestroit

Ladyland's Drive

Artificial Ski Slope

The Sick Mans Path

Bongate Ct   Upp Bongate Gdns   Old Bongate   BONGATE

Forthill Terr   Hume Pl   Stonehill Pl   Forthill Ter   Forthill Ave

Priors Ct   Priors Meadow   Elliot Rd

Meikle Cleuch

Sports Cen

Bank-end

Townfoot Bridge

Priors Road

Hartrigge Road   Hartrigge Cres

Works

Wildcat Wood

Jedburgh Grammar

Pleasance

Park

Waterside

Priors Road

Meadow St

Cairnmount

Willow Ct

Friargate

Jewellers Wynd

High Street   Queen Street

1   12

Springfield Road

Exchange St   Balfour Ct

PO   2   3   10

9 Queens Ct

Canongate Bridge   13

Milfield Gdns   14

Bountrees

Parkside Primary

Oakieknowe Road

Ind Est

Larkhall Burn

4 7   8   11
6   5

CANONGATE   16   15

Sheriff Deans Court Cl

Boundaries

Road

Dunshill Dr

Alder Ave

Skiprunning Burn

Arholl Ct

CASTLEGATE MKT PL

Abbey (rems)

Abbey Pl   Abbey Rd

The Bow

Abbey Ct

Abbey Bridge End

Oxnam Road

Allerton Ct

Avenue

Dounehill

Hunthill

Rowan Road   Beech Wk

Wildcat Cleuch Road

Anton

Castle Terr

NEWCASTLE ROAD

Swimming Pool

Allerton Pl

Blair Avenue

Honeyfield Dr

Howdenburn Drive   Howdenburn Ct

Playing Field

Lochend

Cherry Dean

Hawick   B6358

Jedburgh Castle Jail

Lothian Park

Rugby Ground

Honeyfield Rd

Grieve Ave

Howdenburn Primary

Howden Pk

Howden Ct

Castlewood Cemetery

Galahill

Allerley Well Park

Lothian Road

Howden Drive

Howden Burn

Howden Farm

Antylands

Allars Mill

Bowl Grn

Honeyfield Gro

Brewster Pl

Howden Crescent

Road

Orchard Dene

Cyprus Gro

Allerley Crescent

Allars

Howdenburn Glen

Howden Farm Cottages

Miller's Burn

Lightpipebrae Plantation

Inchbonny Bridge

A68   To Newcastle

Howdenburn Glen

Index to street names can be found overleaf

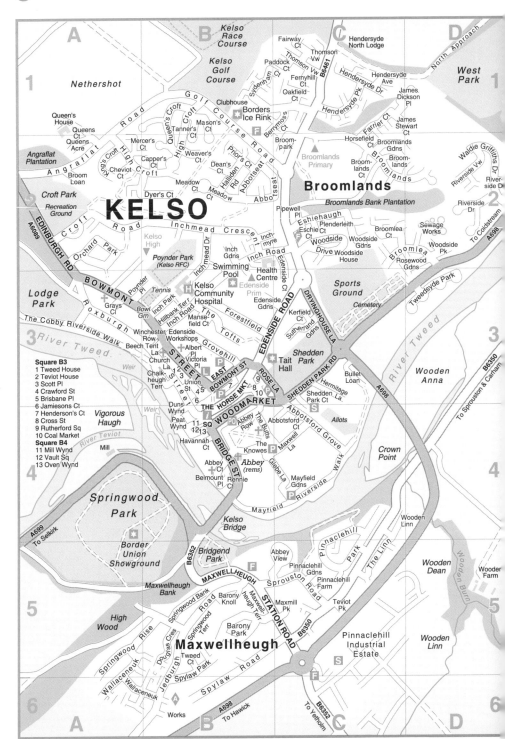

KELSO

Broomlands

Maxwellheugh

Square B3
1 Tweed House
2 Teviot House
3 Scott Pl
4 Crawford St
5 Brisbane Pl
6 Jamiesons Ct
7 Henderson's Ct
8 Cross St
9 Rutherford Sq
10 Coal Market
Square B4
11 Mill Wynd
12 Vault Sq
13 Oven Wynd

dex to Jedburgh

bbey Bridge End	25 B4
bbey Close	25 A4
bbey Place	25 B4
der Avenue	25 D4
lerley Crescent	25 B5
lerton Court	25 B4
lerton Place	25 B4
holl Court	25 A4
alfour Court	25 A3
ankend	25 B3
ankend Path	25 B2
ankend South	25 B2
eech Walk	25 D4
ackhills Close (7)	25 A3
air Avenue	25 B4
ongate	25 B2
ongate Gardens	25 B2
ongate View	25 B2
oundaries	25 B4
ountrees	25 B3
ow, The	25 B4
ewster Place	25 B5
urn Wynd (4)	25 A3
airnmount	25 A3
anongate	25 B3
astle Terrrace	25 A4
astlegate	25 A4
herry Dean	25 D4
ornelius Close (8)	25 A3
own Lane (9)	25 B3
ypress Grove	25 B5
arnley's Close (2)	25 B3
eans Close	25 B3
ounehill	25 C4
uck Row (16)	25 B3
unshill Drive	25 C4
dinburgh Road	25 C1
liot Road	25 C2
xchange Street	25 A3
orthill Avenue	25 B3
orthill Terrace	25 B3
arsgate	25 B3
alahill	25 A4
rahamslaw	25 A3
Close (3)	
ieve Avenue	25 B4
artrigge Crescent	25 C3
artrigge Road	25 C3
eadrig	25 C2
gh Street	25 B3
oneyfield Drive	25 B4
oneyfield Grove	25 B5
oneyfield Road	25 B5
owden Crescent	25 B5
owden Drive	25 C5
owden Farm	25 D5
Cottages	
owden Park	25 C4
owden Road	25 B5
owdenburn Court	25 C4
owdenburn Drive	25 C4
me Place	25 B2
anthill Road	25 C4
dbank Drive	25 B2
dbank Grove	25 B2
wellers Wynd	25 B3
rkhall Burn	25 A3

Ladylands Drive	25 A2
Lanton Road	25 A3
Lothian Road	25 B4
Malestroit Court	25 B2
Market Place	25 A3
Meadow Street	25 B3
Milfield Gardens	25 B3
Newcastle Road	25 B4
Ninian Bell's	25 B3
Close (1)	
Oakieknowe Road	25 C3
Old Bongate	25 B2
Old Bridge End (14)	25 B3
Oldhall Cottages	25 D2
Oldhall Houses	25 D2
Oxnam Road	25 B4
Pleasance	25 B3
Priors Court	25 C2
Priors Meadow	25 C2
Priors Road	25 B3
Queen Mary's	25 B3
Buildings (12)	
Queen Mary's	25 B3
House (11)	
Queen's Court	25 B3
Queens Street	25 B3
Richmond Row (15)	25 B3
Rowan Road	25 D4
Sharplaw Cottages	25 B1
Sharplaw Road	25 B2
Sick Man's Path, The	25 B2
Smith's Wynd (10)	25 B3
Springfield	25 A3
Stonehill Place	25 B2
Totches Baulk	25 A2
Road	
Upper Bongate	25 B2
Gardens	
Upper Nag's Head	25 A3
Close (6)	
Veitch's Close (5)	25 A3
Waterside	25 B3
Well House (13)	25 B3
Wildcat Cleugh	25 A4
Willow Court	25 A3

Index to Kelso

Abbey Court	25 B4
Abbey Row	26 B4
Abbey View	26 C5
Abbotseat	26 B2
Abbotsford Court	26 C4
Abbotsford Grove	26 C4
Albert Place	26 B3
Angraflat Road	26 A2
Barony Knoll	26 B5
Barony Park	26 B5
Beech Tent Lane	26 B3
Belmount Place	26 B4
Berrymoss Court	26 C1
Bowmont Street	26 A3
Bridge Street	26 B4
Brisbane Place (5)	26 B3
Broom Loan	26 A2
Broomlands	26 C2
Broomlands Court	26 C2
Broomlands	26 C2
Gardens	

Broomlea	26 C2
Broomlea Court	26 C2
Broompark	26 C2
Bullet Loan	26 C3
Butts, The	26 B4
Capper's Court	26 B2
Chalkheugh Terrace	26 B3
Cheviot Court	26 A2
Church Lane	26 B3
Coal Market (10)	26 B3
Cobby Riverside	26 A3
Walk, The	
Crawford Street (4)	26 B3
Croft Road	26 A2
Cross Street (8)	26 B3
Dean's Court	26 B2
Douglas Crescent	26 B5
Dryinghouse Lane	26 C3
Duns Wynd	26 B4
Dyer's Court	26 B2
East Bowmont	26 B3
Street	
Edenside Court	26 C2
Edenside Gardens	26 B3
Edenside Road	26 B3
Edinburgh Road	26 A2
Eschie Court	26 C2
Eshiehaugh	26 C2
Fairway Court	26 C1
Farrier Court	26 C1
Fernyhill Court	26 C1
Forestfield	26 B3
Glebe Lane	26 C4
Golf Course Road	26 B1
Grays Close	26 A3
Grovehill	26 B3
Halliden Road	26 B2
Havannah Court	26 B4
Henderson's	26 B3
Court (7)	
Hendersyde	26 C1
Avenue	
Hendersyde Drive	26 C1
Hendersyde Park	26 C1
Hermitage Lane	26 C3
High Croft	26 A2, B2
Hillbank Terrace	26 B3
Horsefield Court	26 C2
Horsemarket	26 B3
Inch Gardens	26 B2
Inch Park	26 B3
Inch Road	26 B2, B3
Inchmead	26 B2
Crescent	
Inchmead Drive	26 B2
Inchmyre	26 B2
James Dickson	26 D1
Place	
James Stewart	26 D1
Court	
Jamiesons	26 B3
Court (6)	
Jedburgh Road	26 B6
Kerfield Court	26 C3
King's Croft	26 A2
Knowes, The	26 B4
Linn, The	26 C5
Mansefield Court	26 B3
Mason's Court	26 B1

Maxmill Park	26 C5
Maxwell Lane	26 C4
Maxwellheugh	26 B5
Maxwellheugh	26 B5
Terrace	
Mayfield Riverside	26 B4
Walk	
Mayfield Gardens	26 C4
Meadow Court	26 B2
Mercer's Court	26 A2
Mill Wynd (11)	26 B4
North Approach	26 D1
Oakfield Court	26 C1
Orchard Park	26 A2
Oven Wynd (13)	26 B4
Paddock Court	26 C1
Peat Wynd	26 B4
Pinnaclehill Farm	26 C5
Pinnaclehill	26 C5
Gardens	
Pinnaclehill Park	26 C5
Pipewell Place	26 C2
Plenderleith Court	26 C2
Poynder Place	26 A3
Prior's Court	26 B2
Queens Acre	26 A2
Queens Court	26 A1
Queen's Croft	26 B2
Rennie Court	26 B4
Riverside Drive	26 D2
Riverside View	26 D2
Rose Lane	26 B3
Rosewood Gardens	26 D2
Roxburgh Street	26 A3
Rutherford	26 B3
Square (9)	
Scott Place (3)	26 B3
Shedden Park Court	26 C3
Shedden Park Road	26 C3
Springwood Bank	26 B5
Springwood Rise	26 A5
Springwood Terrace	26 B5
Sprouston Road	26 B3
Spylaw Park	26 B6
Spylaw Road	26 B6
Square, The	26 B4
Station Road	26 B5
Sutherland Gardens	26 C3
Sydenham Court	26 B1
Tanner's Court	26 B1
Teviot House (2)	26 B3
Teviot Park	26 C5
Thomson View	26 C1
Tofts, The	26 B3
Tweed Court	26 B5
Tweed House (1)	26 B3
Tweedsyde Park	26 D3
Union Street	26 B3
Vault Square (12)	26 B4
Victoria Place	26 B3
Waldie Griffiths Drive	26 D2
Wallaceneuk	26 A6
Weaver's Court	26 B2
Winchester Row	26 B3
Wooden Linn	26 C4
Woodmarket	26 B4
Woodside Drive	26 C2
Woodside Gardens	26 C2
Woodside Park	26 D2

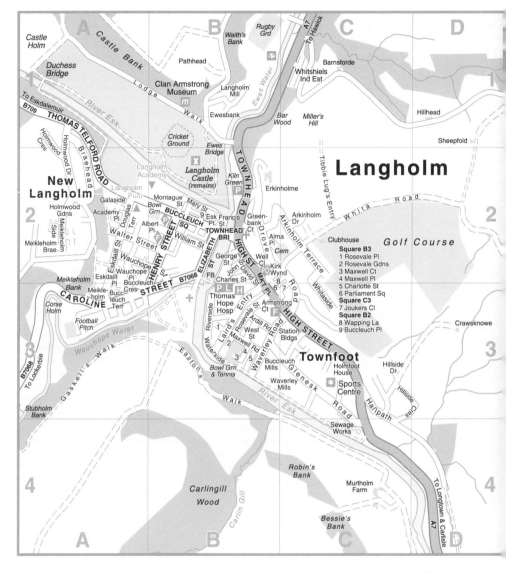

Index to Langholm

		Buccleuch Crescent	A3	Drove Road	B2	Glenesk Road	C
		Buccleuch Mills	B3	Easton's Walk	B3	Greenbank Court	B
Academy Place	A2	Buccleuch Place (9)	B2	Elizabeth Street	B2	Hallpath	C
Albert Place	B2	Buccleuch Square	B2	Esk Place	B2	Henry Street	B
Alma Place	B2	Buccleuch Terrace	A3	Eskdaill Place	A2	High Street	B2, C
Ardill Road	B3	Caroline Street	A3	Eskdaill Street	A2	Hillside Crescent	C
Arkinholm Drive	C2	Charles Street	B2	Francis Street	B2	Hillside Drive	C
Arkinholm Terrace	C2	Charlotte Street (5)	B3	Galaside	A2	Holmfoot House	C
Armstrong Court	B3	David Street	B2	Gaskell's Walk	A3	Holmwood Crescent	A
Braehead	A1	Douglas Terrace	A2	George Street	B2	Holmwood Drive	A

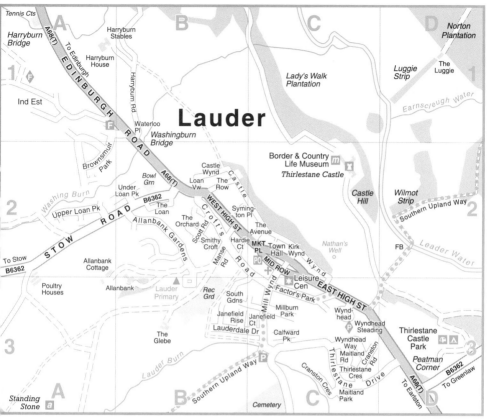

Lauder

olmwood Gardens	A2	Station Buildings	C3	Brownsmuir Park	A2	Mid Row	C2
ohn Street	B2	Thomas Telford Road	A1	Calfward Park	C3	Mill Wynd	C3
oukers Close (7)	C3	Tibbie Lug's Entry	C2	Castle Wynd	B2	Millburn Park	C3
irk Wynd	B2	Townhead Bridge	B2	Cranston	C3	Orchard, The	B2
aird's Entry	B3	Townhead	B2	Crescent		Row, The	B2
odge Walk	A1	Walter Street	A2	Cranston Road	C3	Scott Road	B2
arket Place	B2	Wapping Lane (8)	B2	Croft's Road	B2	Smithy Croft	B2
lary Street	B2	Waterside	B3	East High Street	C3	South Gardens	B3
axwell Court (3)	B3	Wauchope Place	A2	Edinburgh Road	A1	Stow Road	A2
axwell Place (4)	B3	Wauchope Street	A2	Factor's Park	C3	Symington Place	B2
axwell Road	B3	Waverley Mills	B3	Hardie Court	B2	Thirlestane	C3
eikleholm	A3	Waverley Road	B3	Harryburn Road	B1	Crescent	
eikleholm Brae	A2	Well Close	B2	Janefield Court	C3	Thirlestane Drive	C3
eikleholm Side	A2	West Street	B3	Janefield Rise	B3	Under Loan Park	B2
lontague Street	B2	Whita Road	C2	Kirk Wynd	C2	Upper Loan Park	A2
arliament	B3	Whitaside	C3	Lauderdale Drive	B3	Waterloo Place	B1
Square (6)		William Street	B2	Loan, The	B2	West High Street	B2
iverside	B3			Loan View	B2	Wyndhead	C3
osevale	B3	**Index to Lauder**		Maitland Park	C3	Wyndhead Steading	C3
Gardens (2)				Maitland Road	C3	Wyndhead Way	C3
osevale Place (1)	B3	Allanbank Gardens	B2	Manse Road	B2		
osevale Street	B3	Avenue, The	C2	Market Place	C2		

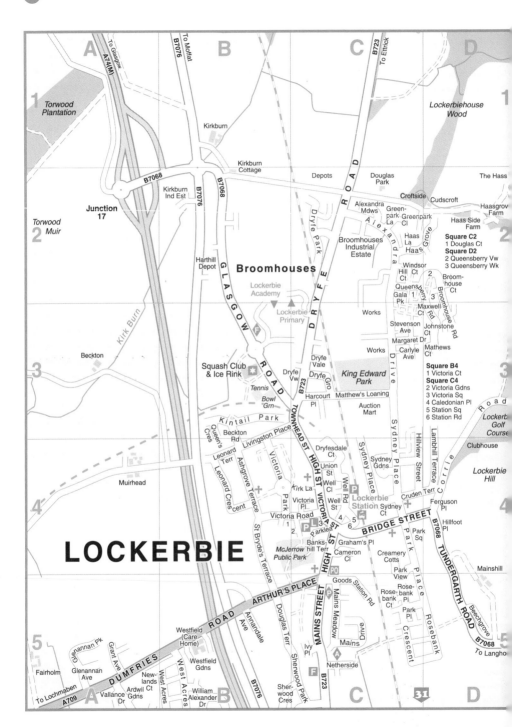

LOCKERBIE

Square C2
1 Douglas Ct
Square D2
2 Queensberry Vw
3 Queensberry Wk

Square B4
1 Victoria Ct
Square C4
2 Victoria Gdns
3 Victoria Sq
4 Caledonian Pl
5 Station Sq
6 Station Rd

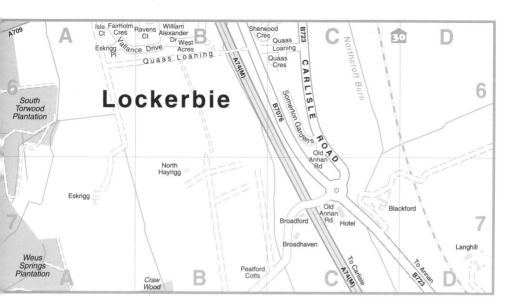

Index to Lockerbie

lexandra Drive	30 C2	Fairholm Crescent	31 A6	Margaret Drive	30 C3	Somerton Gardens	31 C6
lexandra Meadows	30 C2	Ferguson Place	30 D4	Mathews Court	30 D3	Station Road (6)	30 C4
nnandale Avenue	30 B5	Gala Park	30 C2	Matthew's Loaning	30 C3	Station Square (5)	30 C4
rdwil Gardens	30 A5	Glasgow Road	30 B2	Maxwell Court	30 C3	Stevenson Avenue	30 C3
rthur's Place	30 B5	Glenannan Avenue	30 A5	Netherside	30 C5	Sydney Court	30 C4
shgrove Terrace	30 B4	Glenannan Park	30 A5	Newlands Court	30 B5	Sydney Gardens	30 C4
ankshill Terrace	30 C4	Goods Station Road	30 C5	Old Annan Road	31 C7	Sydney Place	30 C3, C4
eckton Road	30 B3	Graham's Place	30 C4	Park Place	30 C4, C5	Townhead Street	30 C3
eechgrove	30 D5	Grant Avenue	30 A5	Park Square	30 C4	Tundergarth Road	30 D4
ridge Street	30 C4	Greenpark Close	30 C2	Park View	30 C4	Union Street	30 C4
roomhouse Court	30 D2	Greenpark Lane	30 C2	Parklea	30 C4	Vallance Drive	30 A5
roomhouse Road	30 D2	Haas Grove	30 C2	Peatford	31 B7	Vallance Drive	31 A6
aledonian	30 C4	Haas Lane	30 C2	Cottages		Victoria Court (1)	30 B4
Place (4)		Harcourt Place	30 C3	Quaas Crescent	31 C6	Victoria Gardens (2)	30 C4
ameron Close	30 C4	High Street	30 C4	Quaas Loaning	31 B6, C6	Victoria Park	30 B4
arlisle Road	31 C6	Hill Court	30 C2	Queen's	30 B3	Victoria Place	30 C4
arlyle Avenue	30 C3	Hillfoot Place	30 D3	Crescent		Victoria Road	30 B4
orrie Road	30 D4	Hillview Street	30 C4	Queensberry	30 C2	Victoria Square (3)	30 C4
reamery Cottages	30 C4	Isle Court	31 A6	Road		Victoria Street	30 C4
ruden Terrace	30 C4	Ivy Place	30 C5	Queensberry	30 D2	Well Close	30 C4
ouglas Court (1)	30 C2	Johnstone Court	30 D3	View (2)		Well Road	30 C4
ouglas Terrace	30 B5	Kintail Park	30 B3	Queensberry	30 D2	Well Street	30 C4
yfe Grove	30 C3	Kirk Lane	30 C4	Walk (3)		West Acres	30 B5
yfe Park	30 C2	Lambhill Terrace	30 D3	Ravens Court	31 B6	West Acres	31 B6
yfe Road	30 C3	Leonard Crescent	30 B4	Rosebank Court	30 C5	Wesfield Gardens	30 B5
yfe Vale	30 C3	Leonard Terrace	30 B4	Rosebank Crescent	30 D5	William Alexander	30 B5
yfe View	30 C3	Livingston Place	30 B4	Rosebank Place	30 C5	Drive	
yfesdale Court	30 C4	Mains Drive	30 C5	St Bryde's Terrace	30 B4	William Alexander	31 B6
umfries Road	30 A5	Mains Meadow	30 C5	Sherwood Crescent	30 B5	Drive	
skrigg Place	31 A6	Mains Street	30 C5	Sherwood Park	30 C5	Windsor Court	30 C2

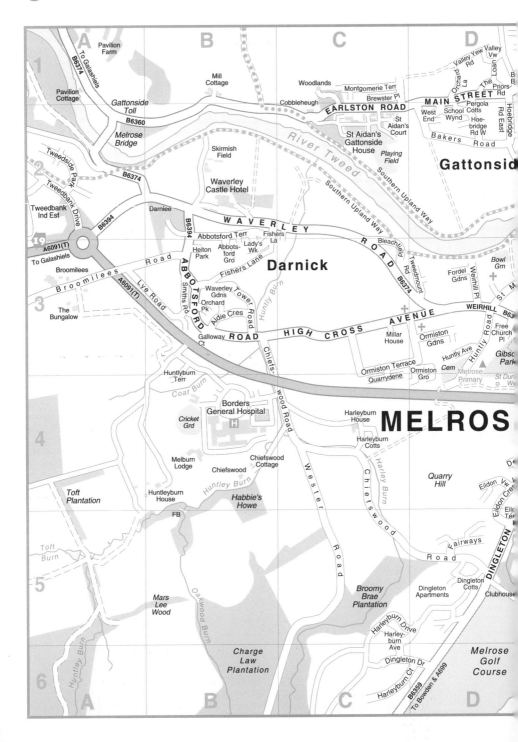

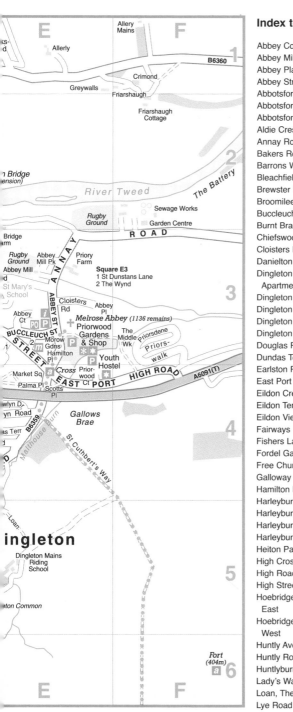

Index to Melrose

Abbey Court	E2	Main Street	D1
Abbey Mill Park	E2	Market Square	E4
Abbey Place	E2	Middle Walk, The	F3
Abbey Street	E2	Millar House	C3
Abbotsford Grove	B3	Monkswood Road	E1
Abbotsford Road	B3	Montgomerie Terrace	C1
Abbotsford Terrace	B2	Morow Gardens	E2
Aldie Crescent	B3	Newlyn Drive	E4
Annay Road	E2	Newlyn Road	E4
Bakers Road	D2	Orchard Lane	D1
Barrons Way	D4	Orchard Park	B3
Bleachfield	C3	Ormiston Gardens	D3
Brewster Place	C1	Ormiston Grove	D3
Broomilees Road	A3	Ormiston Terrace	C3
Buccleuch Street	E2	Palma Place	E4
Burnt Brae	D1	Pergola Cottages	D2
Chiefswood Road	B3, C4	Priors Road	D1
Cloisters Road	E2	Priorsdene	F3
Danielton Cottages	D5	Priorswalk	F3
Dingleton	D5	Priorwood Court	E4
Apartments		Quarrydene	C4
Dingleton Cottages	D5	St Dunstans Lane (1)	E2
Dingleton Drive	C6	St Dunstans Park	E2
Dingleton Loan	D5	St Mary's Road	D3
Dingleton Road	D5	School Wynd	D2
Douglas Road	D4	Scotts Place	E4
Dundas Terrace	E4	Smiths Road	B3
Earlston Road	C2	Tower Road	B3
East Port	E4	Tweedbank Drive	A2
Eildon Crescent	D5	Tweedmount Road	D3
Eildon Terrace	D5	Tweedside Park	A2
Eildon View	D4	Valley View	D1
Fairways	D5	Valley Yew Road	D1
Fishers Lane	B3	Waverley Gardens	B3
Fordel Gardens	D3	Waverley Road	B2
Free Church Place	D3	Weirhill	D3
Galloway Court	B3	Weirhill Place	D3
Hamilton Place	E2	Wembley Terrace	D4
Harleyburn Avenue	C5	West End	D2
Harleyburn Cottages	C4	Wester Road	C4
Harleyburn Court	C6	Wynd, The (2)	E2
Harleyburn Drive	C5		
Heiton Park	B3		
High Cross Avenue	C3		
High Road	F4		
High Street	D3		
Hoebridge Road	D2		
East			
Hoebridge Road	D2		
West			
Huntly Avenue	D3		
Huntly Road	D4		
Huntlyburn Terrace	B3		
Lady's Walk	B3		
Loan, The	D1		
Lye Road	A3		

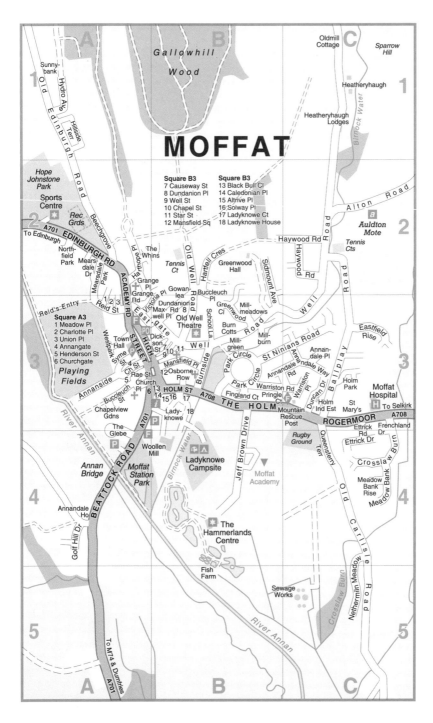

MOFFAT

Square B3
7 Causeway St
8 Dundanion Pl
9 Well St
10 Chapel St
11 Star St
12 Mansfield Sq

Square B3
13 Black Bull Cl
14 Caledonian Pl
15 Altrive Pl
16 Solway Pl
17 Ladyknowe Ct
18 Ladyknowe House

Square A3
1 Meadow Pl
2 Charlotte Pl
3 Union Pl
4 Annangate
5 Henderson St
6 Churchgate

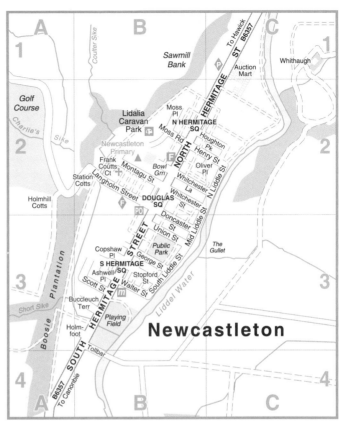

Index to Moffat

Academy Road	A2
Alton Road	C2
Altrive Place (15)	B3
Annandale Place	C3
Annandale Road	C3
Annandale Way	C3
Annangate (4)	A3
Annanside	A3
Ballplay Road	C3
Beattock Road	A4
Beechgrove	A2
Black Bull Close (13)	B3
Buccleuch Place	B2
Buccleuch Street	A3
Burn Cottages	B3
Burnside	B3
Caledonian Place (14)	B3
Causeway Street (7)	B3
Chapel Street (10)	B3
Chapleview Gardens	A3
Charlotte Place (2)	A3
Church Place	A3
Church Street	A3
Churchgate (6)	A3
Crosslaw Burn	C4
Dickson Street	B3
Duncan Drive	C3
Dundanion Place (8)	B3
Dundanion Road	B3
Eastfield Rise	C3
Eastgate	A3
Edinburgh Road	A2
Ettrick Drive	C4
Ettrick Road	C3
Fingland Court	B3
Frenchland Drive	C3
Glebe, The	A4
Golf Hill Drive	A4
Gowanlea	B2
Grange Place	B2
Grange Road	A3
Greenwood Close	B3
Hartfell Crescent	B2
Harthope Place	A2
Haywood Road	C2
Henderson Street (5)	A3
High Street	A3
Hillside Terrace	A1
Holm Park	C3
Holm Street	B3
Holm, The	B3
Hydro Avenue	A1
Jeff Brown Drive	B4
Ladyknowe	B3
Ladyknowe Court (17)	B3
Ladyknowe House (18)	B3
Mansfield Place	B3
Mansfield Square (12)	B3
Maxwell Place	B3
Meadow Bank Rise	C4
Meadow Bank	C4
Meadow Place (1)	A3
Mearsdale Drive	A2
Mearsdale Park	A2
Millburn	B3
Millgreen	B3
Millmeadows	B3
Nethermiln Meadow	C5
Northfield Park	A2
Old Carlisle Road	C4
Old Edinburgh Road	A1
Old Well Road	B2
Osborne Row	B3
Park Circle	B3
Pringle Court	B3
Queensferry Terrace	C4
Rae Street	A3
Reid Street	A3
Reid's Entry	A3
Rogermoor	C3
St Mary's	C3
St Ninians Road	B3
School Lane	B3
Sidmount Avenue	B2
Solway Place (16)	B3
Star Street (11)	B3
Sunnybank	A1
Syme Street	A3
Union Place (3)	A3
Victoria Place	A3
Warriston Place	C3
Warriston Road	B3
Well Road	B3, C3
Well Street (9)	B3
Westpark	A3
Whins, The	A2
Holmhill Cottages	A2
Houghton Park	C2
Langholm Street	B2
Mid Liddle Street	B3
Montagu Street	B2
Moss Place	B2
Moss Road	B2
North Hermitage Square	B2
North Hermitage Street	B2
North Liddle Street	C2
Oliver Place	C2
Scott Street	B3
South Hermitage Square	B3
South Hermitage Street	B3
South Liddle Street	B3
Station Cottages	B2
Stopford Street	B3
Tollbar	B4
Union Street	B3
Walter Street	B3
Whitchester Lane	B2
Whitchester Street	B2

Index to Newcastleton

Ashwell Place	B3
Buccleuch Terrace	B3
Copshaw Place	B3
Doncaster Street	B3
Douglas Square	B2
Frank Coutts Court	B2
George Street	B3
Henry Street	B2
Holmfoot	A3

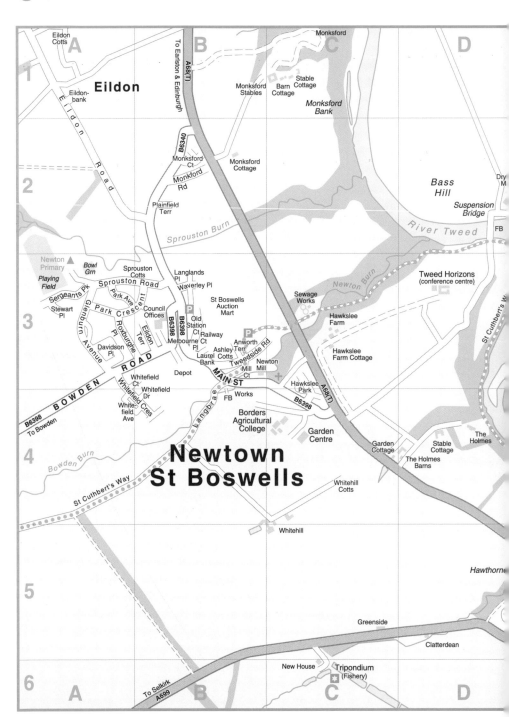

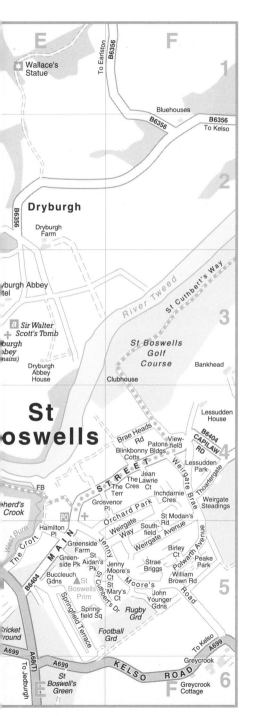

Index to Newtown St Boswells & St Boswells

Anworth Terrace	B3	Sergeants Park	A3
Ashley Cottages	B3	Southfield	F5
Birley Court	F5	Springfield Square	E5
Blinkbonny Cottages	F4	Springfield Terrace	E5
Bowden Road	A4	Sprouston Cottages	B3
Brae Heads Road	F4	Sprouston Road	A3
Buccleuch Chase	D5	Stewart Place	A3
Buccleuch Gardens	E5	Strae Briggs	F5
Capilaw Road	F4	Terrace, The	F4
Crescent, The	F4	Thoartergate	F4
Croft, The	E5	Tweedside Road	B3
Davidson Place	A3	Viewfield	F4
Eildon Cottages	A1	Waverley Place	B3
Eildon Road	A1	Weirgate Avenue	F5
Eildon Terrace	B3	Weirgate Brae	F4
Eildonbank	A1	Weirgate Steadings	F4
Glenburn Avenue	A3	Weirgate Way	F5
Greenside Park	E5	Whitefield Avenue	A4
Grosvenor Place	F4	Whitefield Court	B3
Hamilton Place	E5	Whitefield Crescent	A3
Hawkslee Park	C3	Whitefield Drive	B4
Inchdarnie Crescent	F4	Whitehill Cottages	C4
Jean Lawrie Court	F4	William Brown Road	F5
Jenny Moore's Court	F5		
Jenny Moore's Road	F5		
John Younger Gardens	F5		
Kelso Road	F6		
Langbrae	B4		
Langlands Place	B3		
Laurel Bank	B3		
Lessudden Park	F4		
Main Street (Newton St Boswells)	B3		
Main Street (St Boswells)	E5		
Melbourne Place	B3		
Mill Court	B3		
Monkford Road	B2		
Monksford Court	B2		
Old Station Court	B3		
Orchard Park	F4		
Park Avenue	A3		
Park Crescent	A3		
Patons Buildings	F4		
Peake Park	F5		
Plainfield Terrace	B2		
Polwarth Avenue	F5		
Railway Court	B3		
Roxburghe Place	A3		
St Aidan's Park	E5		
St Cuthbert's Drive	E5		
St Mary's Court	F5		
St Modan's Road	F4		

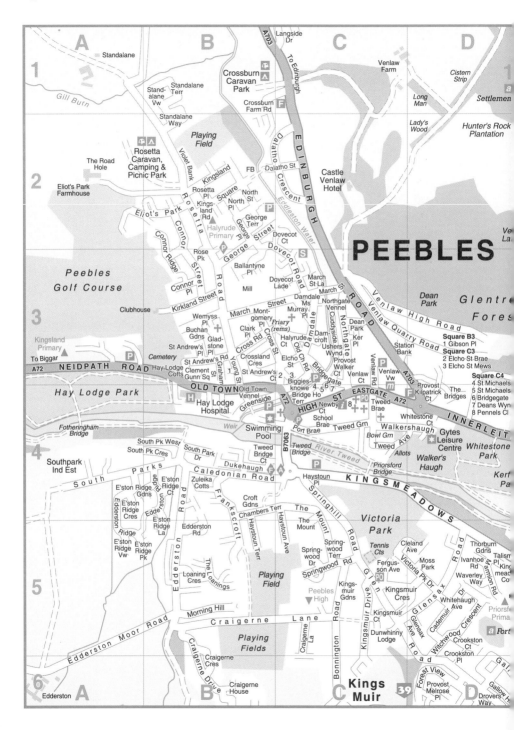

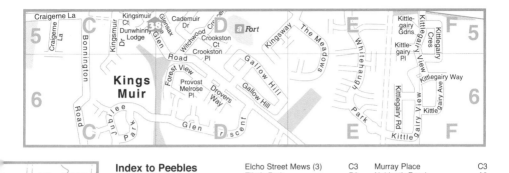

Index to Peebles

Ballantyne Place	B3	Elcho Street Mews (3)	C3	Murray Place	C3
Biggiesknowe	C4	Eliot's Park	B2	Neidpath Road	A3
Bonnington Road	C6	Elm Court	E5	Newby Court	C4
Bridge House Terrace	C4	Fergusson Avenue	C5	North Place	B2
Bridgegate	C3	Forest View	D6	North Street	B2
Bridgegate Court (6)	C4	Frankscroft	B4	Northgate	C3
Bridges, The	D4	Gallow Hill	D6	Northgate Vennel	C3
Buchan Gardens	B3	George Place	B2	Old Church Road	C3
Cademuir Drive	D5	George Street	B3	Old Town	B4
Caledonian Road	B4	George Terrace	B2	Old Town Vennel	B4
Cavalry Park	E5	Gibson Place (1)	B3	Port Brae	C4
Chambers Terrace	B4	Gladstone Place	B3	Provost Kilpatrick Court	D4
Cherry Court	E5	Glen Crescent	D6	Provost Melrose Place	D6
Clark Place	B3	Glen Road	C5	Provost Walker Court	C3
Cleland Avenue	C5	Glensax Avenue	D5	Rose Park	B3
Clement Gunn Square	B3	Glensax Road	D5	Rosetta Place	B2
Connor Place	B3	Greenside	B4	Rosetta Road	B2
Connor Ridge	B2	Halyrude Court	C3	Rowan Court	E5
Connor Street	B2	Hay Lodge Cottages	B3	St Andrew's Court	B3
Craigerne Crescent	B6	Haystoun Avenue	C5	St Andrew's Place	B3
Craigerne Drive	B5, B6	Haystoun Place	C4	St Andrew's Road	B3
Craigerne House	B6	Haystoun Terrace	B5	St Michaels Bank (4)	C4
Craigerne Lane	B5, C5	High Street	C4	St Michaels Wynd (5)	C4
Croft Gardens	B4	Hydro Cottages	E4	School Brae	C4
Crookston Court	D5	Innerleithen Road	D4	South Park Crescent	A4
Crookston Place	D6	Ivanhoe Road	D5	South Park Drive	B4
Cross Road	B3	Janet's Brae Road	E4	South Park West	B4
Cross Street	B3	Jubilee Park	C6	South Parks	A4
Crossburn Farm Road	B1	Ker Place	C3	Springhill Road	C4
Crossland Crescent	B3	Kingsland Road	B2	Springwood Drive	C5
Cuddyside	C3	Kingsland Square	B2	Springwood Road	C5
Dalatho Crescent	C2	Kingsmeadows Cottages	D5	Springwood Terrace	C5
Dalatho Street	C2	Kingsmeadows Gardens	D5	Standalane Terrace	B1
Damcroft	C3	Kingsmeadows Road	C4	Standalane View	B1
Damdale	C3	Kingsmuir Court	C5	Standalane Way	B2
Damdale Mews	C3	Kingsmuir Crescent	C5	Station Bank	C3
Dean Park	C3	Kingsmuir Drive	C5	Talisman Place	D5
Deans Wynd (7)	C4	Kingsmuir Gardens	C5	Thornburn Gardens	D5
Dovecot Court	C2	Kingsway	D5	Tweed Avenue	C4
Dovecot Lade	C3	Kirkland Street	B3	Tweed Brae	C4
Dovecot Road	C3	Kittlegairy Avenue	F6	Tweed Bridge Court	B4
Drovers Way	D6	Kittlegairy Crescent	F5	Tweed Green	C4
Dukehaugh	B4	Kittlegairy Gardens	E5	Ushers Wynd	C3
Eastgate	C4	Kittlegairy Place	E5	Venlaw Court	C3
Edderston Moor Road	A6	Kittlegairy Road	E6	Venlaw High Road	C3
Edderston Ridge	A4, B4	Kittlegairy View	F5, E6	Venlaw Quarry Road	C3
Edderston Ridge Court	B4	Kittlegairy Way	F5	Venlaw Road	C3
Edderston Ridge	A4	Langside Drive	C1	Venlaw View	C3
Crescent		Loaning Crescent	B5	Victoria Park Drive	C5
Edderston Ridge Gardens	B4	Loanings, The	B5	Violet Bank	B2
Edderston Ridge Lane	B4	March Street	B3, C3	Walker'shaugh	C4
Edderston Ridge Park	A5	March Street Lane	C3	Waverley Way	D5
Edderston Ridge View	A5	Marmion Road	D5	Wemyss Place	B3
Edderston Road	B5	Meadows, The	E5	Whitehaugh Avenue	D5
Edinburgh Road	C2	Montgomery Place	B3	Whitehaugh Park	E5
Elcho Street	C3	Morning Hill	B5	Whitestone Court	D4
Elcho Street Brae (2)	C3	Moss Park	D5	Witchwood Crescent	D5
		Mount, The	C4	Young Street	B3
				Zuleika Cottages	B4

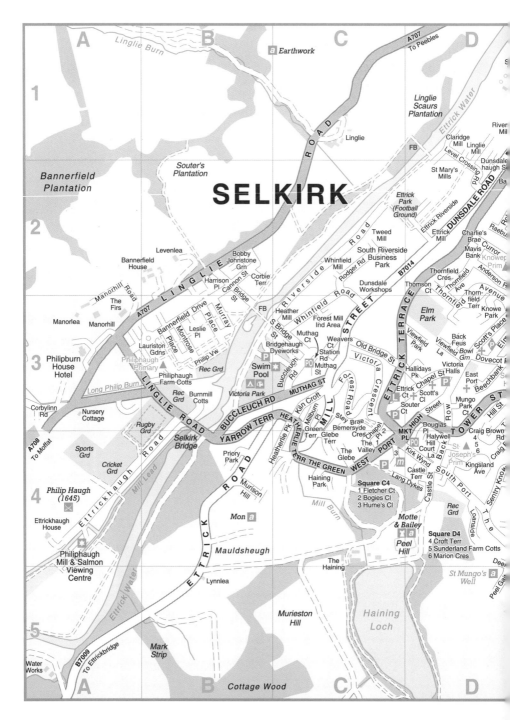

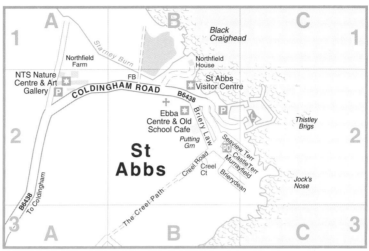

St Abbs

Index to Selkirk

Anderson Road	D2	East Port	D3	Ladywood	E4	Crescent	
Ashybank	E1	Eastfield Road	E2	Lang Dykes	C4	Shawpark Drive	E2
Back Feus	D3	Elm Row	D3	Lauriston Gardens	B3	Shawpark Road	E2
Back Row	D4	Ettrick Court	C3	Leslie Place	B3	Souter Court	C3
Balnagowan Road	D2	Ettrick Riverside	D2	Level Crossing	D1	South Bridge	C3
Bannerfield Drive	B3	Ettrick Road	B5	Road		Street	
Beechbank	D3	Ettrick Terrace	C3	Linglie Road	B3	South Port	D4
Bemersyde	C3	Ettrickhaugh Road	A4	Loan, The	D4	Spion Kop	E1
Crescent		Fairfield Crescent	E2	Loanside	D4	Station Road	C3
Bleachfield Road	D3	Fairfield Drive	E2	Manorhill Road	A3	Stey Brae	C3
Bobby Johnstone		Fletcher Court (1)	C4	Marion	D4	Sunderland Farm	D4
Green	B2	Forrest Road	C3	Crescent (6)		Cottages (5)	
Bogies Close (2)	C4	Gaitschaw Lane	E2	Market Place	C4	Taits Hill	D3
Bridge Street	D3	Glebe Terrace	C4	Mavis Bank	D2	Thirlestane	E2
Bridgelands Road	E1	Glebe, The	C4	Mill Street	C3	Terrace	
Buccleuch Road	B3	Green, The	C4	Millburn Place	C3	Thomson Court	D2
Burnmill Cottages	B3	Goslaw Green	E3	Montrose Place	B3	Thornfield Avenue	D2
Cannon Street	B2	Goslawdales	E3	Mungo Park Court	D3	Thornfield	D2
Castle Street	D4	Green Terrace	C3	Murison Hill	B2	Crescent	
Castle Terrace	D4	Haining Park	C4	Murray Place	B3	Thornfield Terrace	D3
Chapel Place	C3	Hallidays Park	D3	Muthag Court	C3	Tower Street	D3
Chapel Street	D3	Halywell Hill	D4	Muthag Street	C3	Valley, The	C4
Charlie's Brae	D2	Harrison Place	B2	Old Bridge Street	C3	Victoria Crescent	C3
Clifton Road	D3	Heatherlie Park	C4	Peel Gait	E5	Victoria Halls	D3
Corbie Terrace	B2	Heatherlie	C3	Philip View	B3	Viewfield Lane	D3
Corbylinn Road	A3	Terrace		Philiphaugh Farm	B3	Viewfield Park	D3
Court Lane	D4	Heathpark Place	D4	Cottages		Weavers Court	C3
Craig Brown	D4	High School Lane	E3	Priory Park	B4	West Port	C4
Avenue		High Street	D3	Raeburn Lane	E2	Whinfield Road	C3
Craig Brown Road	D4	Hill Street	D3	Raeburn Meadow	D2	Yarrow Terrace	B4
Croft Terrace (4)	D4	Hillside Terrace	E4	Raeburn Place	E2		
Curror Street	D2	Hillview Crescent	D3	Riverside Road	C2	**Index to St Abbs**	
Deer Park	D4	Hume's Close (3)	C4	Roberts Avenue	D2		
Douglas Place	D4	Kiln Croft	C3	Rogers Road	C2	Briery Law	B2
Dovecot Lane	D3	Kingsland	D4	Rosebank Drive	D4	Brierydean	B2
Dovecot Park	D3	Avenue		Russell Place	D3	Castle Terrace	B2
Dunsdale Haugh	D1	Kirk Wynd	D4	Scott Crescent	E3	Coldingham	A2
Dunsdale Road	D4	Knowe Park	D3	Scott's Close	D3	Road	
Dunsdalehaugh	D2	Ladylands Drive	D4	Scott's Brae	D3	Creel Court	B2
Square		Ladylands	D4	Sentry Knowe	D4	Creel Road	B2
		Terrace		Shawburn Road	D2	Murrayfield	B2
		Ladyschaw Drive	E2	Shawpark	E3	Seaview Terrace	B2

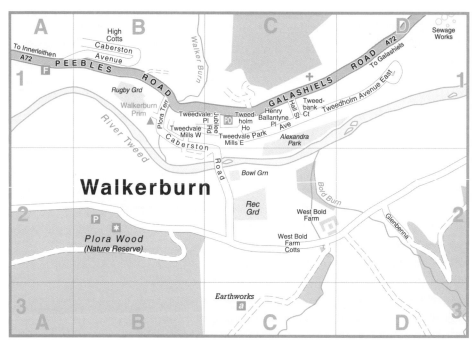

Walkerburn

Index to Walkerburn

Caberston Avenue	B1
Caberston Road	B1
Galashiels Road	C1
Glenbenna	D2
Hall Street	C1
Henry Ballantyne Place	C1
High Cottages	B1
Jubilee Road	C1
Park Avenue	C1
Peebles Road	A1
Plora Terrace	B1
Tweedbank Court	C1
Tweedholm Avenue East	C1
Tweedholm House	C1
Tweedvale Mills East	C1
Tweedvale Mills West	B1
Tweedvale Place	B1
West Bold Farm Cottages	C2

Index to Berwick-upon-Tweed

Adams Drive	7 F9
Albert Place	5 F5
Albert Road	7 H9
Alderbush Close	6 D9
Anderson Court (6)	7 F6
Askew Crescent	7 F8
Ava Lodge	5 E4
Avenue, The	7 G6
Bank Hill	5 F5
Bay Terrace	7 G6
Bede Avenue	5 E3
Bell Tower Park	5 F5
Billendean Road	7 F8
Billendean Terrace	7 F8
Blackhall Court	7 E10
Blakewell Gardens	7 E6
Blakewell Lane	7 E6
Blakewell Street	7 E6
Blenheim Place	7 H9
Bowers Crescent	7 E6
Braeside	7 E9
Brass Bastion	5 E1
Breakneck Steps	5 E5
Brewery Bank	7 E7
Brewery Lane	7 E7
Brickfield Lodge	7 E9
Bridge Court	7 E6
Bridge End	7 F6
Bridge Street	7 F6
Bridge Terrace	7 F6
Brucegate	5 F5
Callers Court	6 D9
Camphill Cottages	4 B2
Carrick Close	5 E3
Castle Drive	5 E4
Castle Terrace	4 D4
Castlegate	5 F5
Castlegate Court (3)	5 F5
Cemetery Lane	7 E9
Chapel Street	5 F5
Chiltern Close	6 D9
Church Road	7 E7
Church Street	7 F6
Cleet Court	7 G6
Clove Court	6 D9
Coastguard Cottages	7 G6
College Place	5 F5
Commercial Road	7 G8
Cornhill Road	6 C8
Cornwall Avenue	6 C9
Countess of Buchan Way	5 E3
Cow Road	7 H9
Coxons Lane	5 F5
Crawford's Alley	5 F5
Crescent, The	7 H9
Crispin Road	5 E3
Croft, The	6 C9
Crosthwaite Terrace	7 F8
Dean Drive	7 E8, E9
Devon Terrace	7 G6
Dewars Lane	7 F6
Dock Road	7 F7
Douglas Close	5 E3
Drivers Lane (6)	7 F6
Duns Road	4 B3, C3
East Ord Farm Cottages	6 B8
East Ord Gardens	6 B9
East Street	7 G8
Eastcliffe	7 G9
Easter Wynd (5)	7 F6
Eastern Lane	7 F6
Eildon View	7 E10
Elms, The	4 D4
Etal Road	6 D10
Etal Road	7 E8
Etal Way	7 E9
Falloden Terrace	7 F8
Farne Road	7 F8
Fetter's Lane	7 F7
Ford Court (9)	7 F6
Foul Ford (10)	7 F6
Freemens Court	5 F5
Gallow Knowe	5 E4
Glamis Hill	5 E3
Glenside Park	6 B9
Golden Square	7 F6
Goldstone	6 D9
Grand Loaning	4 A1
Grange Road	4 D3
Grangeburn Close	6 D9
Green, The	6 B9
Greenside Avenue	5 F5

43

Greenway	6 C9	Millfield Place	6 B8	St Mary's Place (1)	5 F5	Windmill Way North	4 D1
Greenwood	6 D8	Mordington Avenue	6 D9	Sally Port	7 F6	Windmill Way West	4 D1
Grove Gardens	7 E8	Mount Road	7 F7	Sandgate	7 F6	Woolmarket	7 F6
Grove Gardens South	7 E9	NER Cottages	7 E6	Sandstell Road	7 G8	Woolmarket Mews	7 F6
Halidon Terrace	4 C3	Ness Street	7 G6	Sanson Close	6 D9	Yard Heads	7 E6
Hallowstell View	7 G8	New Road	7 F6	School Lane	7 G8	Yarrow Close	6 D8
Harcar Court	6 D9	Newfields	5 E2	Scott's Place	5 F5		
Hatters Lane	5 F5	North Greenwich	7 H8	Sea Road	7 H8	**Index to Galashiels**	
Hawthorne Crescent	7 E9	Road		Sea View	5 F3		
Henderson Court	7 F7	North Road	5 E3	Seaview Cottages	7 H10	Abbots Place	18 F6
Hide Hill	7 F6	Northumberland	5 F4	Seafield Place	7 H9	Abbotsferry Road	19 J7
High Cottages	7 H9	Avenue		Shielfield Terrace	7 E8	Abbotsford Court	17 E5
High Greens	5 F5	Northumberland	7 F8	Sidey Court	5 F5	Abbotsford Place	18 F6
Highcliffe	7 G9	Road		Silver Street	7 F6	Abbotsford Road	17 F5
Hillcrest	6 B8	Oil Mill Lane (11)	7 F6	South Greenwich	7 H9	Abbotsford Road	18 G8
Hillside Lodge	7 E9	Ord Drive	7 E6	Road		Abbotsford Terrace	18 F6
Hillside	7 E9	Ord Road	6 C8	Spittal Hall Place	7 G8	Abbotslea	19 J7
Hiveacres Road	6 D9	Osborne Cottages	6 C8	Spittal Hall Road	7 G8	Abbotsview Court	18 H7
Homebank	6 C8	Osborne Crescent	7 E6	Springdale	7 E9	Abbotsview Drive	18 H7
Howick Terrace	7 F8	Osborne Place	7 E7	Springfield Park	6 C9	Abbotsview Gardens	18 H7
Infirmary Square	5 F5	Osborne Road	7 E7	Springhill Lane	7 E10	Abbotsview Lane	18 H7
Islestone Court	6 D9	Oval, The	7 E8	Stanley Close	6 C9	Albert Place	17 E5
Ivinson Road	6 D8	Palace Green	7 F6	Stephenson Court	7 E10	Anfield Gardens	18 F6
Ivy Place	5 F5	Palace Street	7 F6	Stott Court	7 E10	Aster Cour	19 J5
James Place	7 G8	Palace Street East	7 F6	Summerhill Terrace	5 E4	Balmoral Avenue	16 C5
Kiln Hill	7 E7	Parade	5 G5	Sunnyside Crescent	7 F8	Balmoral Drive	16 C5
King James Court	7 F6	Parade School	5 F5	Sunnyside Cut	7 F9	Balmoral Place	16 D4
Kings Mount	5 E1	Mews		Sunnyside Mews	7 F9	Balmoral Road	16 C5
Knivestone Court	6 D9	Parkside	7 E8	Swanston Mews (4)	5 F5	Balmoral Terrace	16 C5
Knowe Head	7 E7	Pastures, The	6 D8	Temperance Terrace	5 F5	Balnakiel Terrace	16 B2
Ladywell Place	7 E7	Paxton Road	4 B5	Thornton Gate	6 C8	Bank Close (4)	17 E4
Ladywell Road	7 E7	Paxton Road	6 B6	Tower Road	7 F7	Bank Court (3)	17 E4
Lamb Court	7 E10	Percy Terrace	5 F4	Turret Gardens	7 E8	Bank Street	17 E4
Lees Lane	7 F7	Pier Road	7 F6	Tweed Close	6 C8	Bank Street	17 E4
Lindisfarne Gardens	6 C9	Prince Edward Road	7 E6	Tweed Street	5 F5	Brae (1)	
Loaning Meadows	5 E2	Princes Opens (1)	7 G8	Union Brae	7 E6	Barr Road	17 E5
Longstone View	7 G6	Princes Street	7 G8	Union Park Road	7 E6	Beech Avenue	17 H5
Lord's Mount	5 F5	Prior Road	7 E9	Valley View	7 E9	Beechbank Place	17 E4
Lovaine Terrace	5 F4	Prior View	7 E9	Violet Terrace	5 F5	Beeches, The	19 K7, K8
Love Lane	7 F6	Promenade	7 H8	Walkergate	5 F5	Birks View	16 C3
Lovers Walk	7 F6	Pudding Lane	7 E6	Wallace Green	5 F5	Blakehope Court	19 K7
Low Greens	5 F5	Quay Walls	7 F6	Warkworth Terrace	5 F4	Bluebell Lane	19 J5
Magdalene Drive	5 E3	Railway Cottages	6 B9	Waterloo Place	7 G8	Blynlee Lane	16 B2
Main Street	7 E7	Railway Street	5 E5	Waugh Square (8)	7 F6	Boleside Road	18 H8
(Berwick)		Ravensdowne	7 G6	Weddels Court (13)	7 F6	Botany Lane	16 D4
Main Street	7 G8, H9	River Dene	7 E6	Weddels Lane (12)	7 F6	Bow Butts (8)	17 E5
(Spittal)		Riverside Road	7 E6	Well Close Square	5 F5	Bow Butts Close (9)	17 E5
Mansfield Road	6 D9	Riverview Park	7 G8	Well Road	7 F7	Brawlands Brae	17 E5
Marygate	7 F6	Roberts Lodge	7 E10	Well Square	7 F7	Bridge Place	16 D4
Meadow Dale	6 D9	Roddam Court	6 D9	Wellington Terrace	7 F6	Bridge Street	17 E4
Meadow Gardens	6 D9	Rotary Way	6 B8	West End	7 E6	Bridgend Cottages	19 L6
Meadow Grange	5 E3	Rowntree Avenue	7 F8	West End Court	7 E6	Brier Lane	19 J5
Meadow Hill	4 C3	St Aidan's Road	5 E3	West End Place	7 E6	Bristol Terrace	16 C2
Meadow Rigg	6 C9	St Andrews	5 F5	West End Road	7 E6	Broadlee Bank	19 K7
Meadowlands	6 C9	Place (2)		West Street (Berwick)	7 F6	Brock Bank	19 K7
Meadows, The	5 E3	St Andrew's Road	5 E3	West Street (Spittal)	7 G8	Broom Drive	19 J5
Meeting House	7 G8	St Bartholomew's	7 G8	Westfield Avenue	5 F4	Buckholm Mill Brae	16 C2
Lane (2)		Crescent		Westfield Road	5 E4	Buckholm Mill	16 C2
Megstone Court	6 D9	St Cuthbert's Road	5 E3	Whiteadder Close	6 D9	Cottages	
Middle Street	7 G8	St George's Road	5 E3	Whitesand Close	6 D9	Carlin Court	19 K7
Mill Strand	7 E7	St Helen's Terrace	7 H8	Windsor Crescent	5 E4	Carry Weil,The	19 K7
Mill Wharf (1)	7 E7	St Katherine's Place	6 B9	Windmill Way East	5 E1	Catrail Road	16 C3

Name	Ref	Name	Ref	Name	Ref	Name	Ref
Cemetery Road	18 G6	Glenfield Crescent	17 G5	Larchbank Street	18 G6	Rose Court	17 H5
Channel Street	17 E4	Glenfield Road West	17 F5	Larkspur Court	19 J5	Rosebank Place	16 D4
Chapel Street	17 E4	Glenfield Road East	17 G5	Laurel Grove	17 H5	Roxburgh House	16 D4
Cherry Park	19 L7	Glenfield Terrace	17 G5	Lawyers Brae	17 E5	Court	
Church Bank	17 E5	Gorse Lane	19 J5	Lee Brae	16 C2	Roxburgh Place	16 D4
Church Square (7)	17 E5	Green Street	17 E4	Lintburn Place	16 D4	Roxburgh Street	16 D4
Church Street	17 E5	Greenbank Street	17 F5	Lintburn Street	16 D4	St Andrew Street	16 D4
Cochrane Place	18 F6	Gun Knowe Bank	19 K7	Little Dan Avenue	16 B2	St John Street	17 E5
Coopersknowe	19 K5	Haining Drive	19 K6	Livingstone Place	16 D5	Sanderson Court	16 D3
Crescent		Hall Place	16 D4	Loch View	19 K7	Scott Crescent	17 E5
Cornmill Court (6)	17 E5	Hall Street	16 D4	Lochend	19 K7	Scott Street	16 D4
Cornmill Square	17 E5	Halliburton Place	16 C2	Low Buckholmside	16 D3	Shielwood Court	19 K7
Cotgreen Road	19 K7	Halliburton Terrace	16 D3	Lowood Park	19 J7	Sime Place	17 E4
Craigpark Gardens	17 E5	Hareshaw Bank	19 K7	Lucy Sanderson	18 G6	Stable Cottages	19 L6
Craw Wood	19 L7	Hawthorn Road	17 H5	Cottage Homes (2)		Stable Gardens	19 K5
Croft Street	17 F5	Hayward Drive	18 F6	Magdala Terrace	16 C2	Stanley Street	16 D4
Currie Road	17 E4, F5	Hazeldean	16 D4	Manse Court	16 C4	Station Brae	17 E4
Dale Street	18 G6	Heather Court	19 J5	Manse Lane	16 C3	Stirling Place	17 E4
Darghai Lane	16 C3	Heatheryett Drive	17 E3	Manse Place	16 C3	Stirling Street	17 E4
Davidsons Place	18 G6	Heathery Rig	19 J7	Manse Street	16 C3	Stobshaw Place	19 K6
Dean Street	16 C4	High Buckholmside	16 D3	Marigold Bank	17 H5	Stobshaw Terrace	19 K6
Douglas Bridge	17 E4	High Road	17 E4	Marigold Drive	19 J5	Talisman Avenue	17 H5
Douglas Place	18 F6	High Street	16 D4	Market Street	17 E4	Tea Street	17 E5
Douglas Street	17 F5	Hill Street	17 F5	Marmion Road	19 J6	Thistle Street	16 D4
Duke Street	16 C3	Hillside Drive	16 B1	Maryfield Gardens	16 D3	Thornbank Street	17 F5
Easter Langlee	19 K5	Hollybush Road	16 D5	Meigle Street	16 C4	Torwoodlee Road	16 B2
Cottages		Honeylees Drive	19 K7	Meigle View	16 C4	Tulley Court	17 F5
Eildon Lodge	19 K5	Huddersfield Street	17 F5	Melrose Road	17 F4	Tweed Crescent	18 G6
Gardens		Hunter's Bridge Road	16 D3	Melrose Road	19 J5	Tweed Grove	18 G6
Eildon Street	16 C4	Ida Hayward Cottage	18 G6	Mill Park	16 B2	Tweed Road	18 G6, H6
Ellwyn Crescent	17 F4	Homes (1)		Mossilee Crescent	16 C4	Tweed Terrace	18 G6
Ellwyn Terrace	17 F4	Island Street	16 D3	Mossilee Farm	16 B5	Tweedbank	19 L7
Elm Grove	17 E5	Johnstons Close	17 E4	Cottages		Avenue	
Elm Row	17 E5	Jura Drive	19 L7	Mossilee Road	16 C4	Tweedbank Drive	19 K8, L6
Essenside Drive	19 K6	Kenilworth Avenue	18 H6	Neidpath Court	19 K6	Tweedbank View	19 L7
Essenside Place	19 K6	Killie Croft	19 L7	Nether Road	18 H6	Tweedside Park	19 M7
Florentina Way	16 B2	Killie Court	19 K7	Netherbank	18 G7	Union Street	16 D4
Forebrae Park	17 E4	Kilknowe Place	16 B3	Netherview	18 H7	Victoria Street	16 D4
Forest Avenue	16 D5	King Street	16 C3	Netherdale Brae	18 G6	Waitknowe	18 G6
Forest Crescent	16 C5	Kingsknowe Drive	18 H7	Oakwood	16 D5	Terrace	
Forest Gardens	16 C4	Kingsknowe Gardens	18 H7	Oatlands Terrace	18 F6	Wakefield Court	17 F5
Forest Hill	16 C4	Kingsknowe Place	18 H7	Overhaugh Street	17 E4	Waverley Place	18 G6
Forest Place	16 C5	Kingsknowes	18 H7	Park Street	17 E4	Weavers Linn	19 K7
Forest Road	16 D5	Cottages		Parsonage Road	18 F6	Westwood	16 B2
Gala Lane	17 E4	Kingsknowes Village	18 G6	Paterson Street	18 F6	Gardens	
Gala Park	16 D4	Kirk House	16 D4	Paton Street	17 E5	Wheatlands Road	16 B2
Gala Park Court	16 D4	Kirkbrae	16 D4	Plumtree Place	16 C3	Whin Court	19 J5
Gala Park	17 E4	Knowepark Gardens	16 C3	Plumtreehall Brae	16 C2	Wilder Place	16 D3
Gardens (5)		Ladhope Bank	16 D3	Primrose Bank	19 J5	Wilderhaugh Court	16 D3
Gala Park Place	16 D4	Ladhope Crescent	17 E3	Princes Street	16 D3	Wilderhaugh Street	16 D3
Gala Park Road	17 E4	Ladhope Drive	17 E3	Pringle Lane	16 B2	William Law	16 A1
Gala Terrace	17 E5	Ladhope Vale	17 E4	Queen Elizabeth	19 K5	Gardens	
Galabank Street	17 F5	Lady Moss	19 J7	Drive		Windyknowe Road	16 C3
Galafoot Lane	19 J6	Langhaugh	17 F5	Queen Elizabeth	19 L5	Winston Place	19 J6
Galafoot Road	19 J7	Crescent		Square		Winston Road	19 J5
Galahill Crescent	18 E6	Langhaugh	17 F5	Queen Street	16 C3	Wood Street	16 B2
Gibson's Close (2)	17 E4	Gardens		Redpath Crescent	19 K5	Woodlee	16 B2
Gill's Close	17 E4	Langhaugh Lane	17 F5	Riddle Dumble Park	16 C4	Woodside Drive	16 C3
Glebe Place	17 E5	Langlee Avenue	18 H6	Riverside Drive	19 J7	Woodside Place	16 C2
Glendinning Terrace	16 D2	Langlee Drive	17 H5	Roberts Court	17 E3	Woodstock Avenue	18 H6
Glenfield Avenue	17 G5	Langlee Road	18 H6	Roberts Grove	17 E3	Woodstock Road	18 H6
Glenfield Court	17 F5	Larch Grove	17 H5	Roger Quin Gardens	18 G7	Wylies Brae	17 F4